W9-AVN-251

A WIDOW'S ODYSSEY

From Depression to Rejuvenation

JANET JACKSON CRAWFORD

iUniverse, Inc.
New York   Bloomington

A Widow's Odyssey
From Depression to Rejuvenation

iUniverse books may be ordered through booksellers or by contacting:

iUniverse
1663 Liberty Drive
Bloomington, IN 47403
www.iuniverse.com
1-800-Authors (1-800-288-4677)

Because of the dynamic nature of the Internet, any Web addresses or links
contained in this book may have changed since publication and may no longer be
valid. The views expressed in this work are solely those of the author and do not
necessarily reflect the views of the publisher, and the publisher hereby disclaims
any responsibility for them.

ISBN: 978-1-4502-3877-9 (sc)
ISBN: 978-1-4502-3876-2 (dj)
ISBN: 978-1-4502-3875-5 (ebook)

Library of Congress Sontrol Number: 2010908939

Printed in the United States of America

iUniverse rev. date: 07/08/2010

Dedicated to every widowed person

I want to sincerely thank my family for making such a huge effort to help me during a very trying period. Their love for their father was mirrored in all they did to make him comfortable. He was never alone. Without their love and kindness toward both of us, I would have found my great loss far more difficult to bear.

For the last twenty years of our marriage, my husband Richard (Dick) and I journeyed much of the world, 'on roads less traveled', holding each other's hand. Dick often remarked, "Expect nothing and be pleasantly surprised." One day, we came to a road that ended. A smaller road went to the left and another to the right. We didn't say goodbye because we were sure our roads would meet again…..and perhaps they will. Now I walk a road that is unfamiliar, frightening, difficult, heartbreaking and devastating, but I cannot turn back and wherever Dick is, he can never be there, in person, to hold my hand or join me in the delights of life. Someone recently remarked, "We face challenges, but we face them best when we face them together." My children and friends, helped me meet the challenges I now face and because of them, I am able, more and more, to face them alone and with growing confidence and pleasure.

PREFACE

How does one deal with death? For years I have watched death scenes in movies. I shed tears as did most of the audience, yet within a minute, the grief seems dispelled. The characters go on with their lives. This is what I expected. Movies dwell much longer on other parts of life, seldom on the long term effects of death. Even widowed people hide their grief as if it was some sign of weakness. Close relatives and friends seldom know the despair this person is going through.

In real life it is a process that no one can imagine. This story is unfortunately true. It will be true for all of us who are left behind. The gift of life has a little ribbon attached to it, and none of us knows how long that ribbon is. We must treasure the company of those we love and expect grief when those individuals leave us. This story may be read as any story is read—a story of one person's struggle with death and the equal struggle to come to grips with this reality.

For someone who has lost a partner, this book may help them understand that what he or she is going through has a commonality. It will allow them to see that they are not alone in their grief. Each person experiences stages in the process of grieving, even if they vary in length with each individual. This story may help a person know what to expect as they struggle to overcome the heartbreak.

This book may also serve as a guide to those who face the prospects of losing a loved one. If one has some knowledge of what lies ahead, it is far better than coming face to face with devastating and bewildering grief, as I did. It is not a solution. There are none, but realizing that others have suffered, yet struggled through, can create in each of us a source of strength.

PART ONE

Disbelief…Bewilderment…Dismay…Despair…
Helplessness…Depression

Old Dog Trey's ever faithful
Grief cannot drive him away
He's gentle, he is kind
You'll never never find
A better friend than Old Dog Trey

Written by Stephen Foster, a byline of Dick Crawford

CHAPTER ONE
THE PHONE CALL TO AIX EN PROVENCE

"Je suis desolee. Votre fille est dans le telephone."

"Hi Mom."

"Bonjour, Laurie, comment ca va?" I responded, totally delighted to speak French yet disoriented from being suddenly awakened. My heart began to race as I quickly realized that this was not a phone call for a pleasant chat—no silvery thread of laughter in response to my French. I knew my daughter intimately; unlike me, she would be very aware of the nine hour time difference. With her very first words and the tone of her voice, it was obvious that something was very wrong at home.

"Mom," she hesitated, "Dad told me not to call you. He didn't want to spoil your dream. He wanted you to stay in France…but the doctor told me to call you because he said Dad may not live for more than a few days. You have to come home right away." Her voice trailed off, reluctant to give me the news and also break the promise she had made to her father.

"Of course, Laurie, I'll see what I can do. My ticket is for the first of November." I stammered a meaningless response, suddenly experiencing what shock must feel like. I was struck dumb, totally incapable of imagining how to make arrangements for quickly returning home. Not only that, my thoughts about everything evaporated into a feeling of floating in a vacuum.

"He has a dissected aorta twelve inches long. Do you know what that means?"

The vacuum burst into large fragments. I felt a surge of emotion that came from somewhere in my chest and moved up through the back of my neck. Feeling cold and hot at the same time, I heard Laurie say "dissected aorta" but didn't know for sure what it meant. Later, I would be able to recite an explanation as if I were a professional. I could not imagine Dick in any way but as he had always been—his deep voice that people over the phone could recognize before he said more than two words, his strong hug, his warm hands… He always had been healthy. I could not believe he was near death. Yet doctors don't use such strong words unless there is a profound reason. It wasn't possible. I insisted in my own mind that they must be wrong.

———————

Three weeks before, I had carefully pulled my favorite duffle bag down the attic's folding stairs. If you looked closely at that bag, you could see the scars of wear from being tossed onto conveyer belts or shoved into tight compartments. The handle had divorced itself and had to be repaired while Dick and I were in Southern India. One corner of the bag was glued near the area where the wheels were attached. Why I continued to use it was a mystery to some; but somehow, this bag represented the memories and excitement of distant places. I noticed some sand from previous travels in the bottom, but didn't bother to take the bag outside and give it a good shake.

"Let's see. These always travel well, don't wrinkle and dry quickly," I mused as I pulled two khaki pants from the drawer. One pair, with lots of pockets was ideal, with places for the passport and flight information, a small pocket for coins, and another for the digital camera. The best thing about this pair of pants was the elastic drawstring at the bottom of the legs. I could drop my pants over a foreign toilet hole and not have them go past my ankles into mud or heaven knows! I was not a classy dresser; my lifestyle of being with dogs, cats and horses made me a "tom boy." The sweat shirts carried gardening stains and oil paint from my artwork. My days were too full to consider haute couture, too busy living the life I loved.

I typically started packing long before departure. This trip promised to be different, and I was terribly excited about it. I tried to imagine what clothing I would need for a whole month in Provence and I was having a hard time deciding what clothes I should take. Every trip has its unknown elements—weather concerns, the amount of money to take along and gifts for my hosts. The day before I left, I still felt unprepared. Unlike most of our trips where Dick and I went together, this was going to be radically different. I would be traveling alone, not only to San Francisco, but to France. I would be staying with a French family that I had never met.

In the evening before my departure, I let out a big sigh, leaving my bulging bag lying on the floor by the patio door in the bedroom. I walked into the living room where Dick was engrossed in a football game and I sat down beside him. Football was great to watch, but I always seemed too busy doing other things.

Watching TV was not high on my priority list. Moving closer to him, I automatically placed my head on his shoulder.

"I'm going to miss you," I murmured, kissing his ear and placing my hand near his back, a back that craved to be rubbed, all hours of the day and night. He moved forward on the sofa so I would have plenty of room, anticipating five minutes of back rubbing. I had other thoughts on my mind so the back rub was pretty haphazard.

"There won't be that much to do in October. You just have to let the dogs out in the morning and make sure the cat comes in at night." I surely had gone over these words before. It was like packing. I just needed to rehearse the procedure, as if Dick were a stranger taking care of everything. My horse, Hussy, was going to the stable while I was gone, so he didn't have to worry about her.

"Is there anything I'm forgetting?" I half-whispered as I nuzzled my nose next to the soft fuzz on the edge of his ear. "Will you be all right?"

"Hell, I take better care of myself when you're not here," he retorted. I wondered why, since I did my best to keep him happy and healthy. I hoped I had succeeded. We had been married for over a half century and he had never been sick. I made sure that Dick retired from the stress of our veterinary practice when he was fifty. We had moved to Oregon, mostly to please me, since I was determined not to spend another winter in Wisconsin. In Oregon, I cajoled Dick into hiking and cross country skiing, wanting him to stay young, after experiencing the death of my father when he was only forty-eight years old.

Still I wished Dick weighed less and exercised more. His brain usually got the workout as he struggled for hours with the hardest Sudoku he could find. I looked at one occasionally and shook my head. I loved the *results* of my hobbies, like a painting, quilt or the vegetable and flower gardens. I rode my horse several times a week and trained my dogs to perform in agility shows. Dick would simply finish a Sudoku and toss it in a wastebasket!

All conversation stopped as Richard screamed his approval, when a galloping player threw himself into the air for a touchdown. He laughed, "That was a good one! The Bears are ahead by a touchdown!" You can take the boy away from Chicago, but you can't take Chicago away from the boy. Dick was born and raised there—a die-hard Bears' fan.

"I guess I'm nervous because this is the first time I have driven to our friend's place on my own. I keep hoping that I won't make a mistake and end up in San Francisco or Oakland somewhere!" My thoughts were decidedly not on the ball game.

"Oh, you'll do fine. I'll get you a map and directions from the internet. Just read them over and take them along with you. If I can do it, so can you. Just take your time, leave early so you miss the rush hours. It will take you six hours if you stop in Williams for a snack and gas." Dick had always been so supportive of me.

Traveling in high speed traffic requires great attention and swift action to make sure one is in the right lane at the right time. I admired Dick's ability to navigate the route with aplomb, but it wasn't a chore I especially wanted to tackle. As a passenger, I hadn't paid close enough attention to every turn, every change from one Interstate to another. I secretly wanted him to come with me, at least as far as the Ford's house. I hated to leave him, even if I joyously anticipated spending a month in France. For the last twenty years I had been trying to increase my knowledge of French and hoped that there might be an opportunity to immerse myself in the language. Just practicing out of a book made it difficult to truly remember little more than just the basics of the language. At last, I had this long awaited opportunity, but one that would take me away from Dick.

Still dwelling on the harrowing possibilities of the car trip, I relieved my anxiety on a few more minutes of Dick's back rub. In spite of my fears, I looked forward to continuing our ritual of driving to the Ford's house at the beginning of each overseas trip. The drive took most of a day, but it was much cheaper and easier to fly overseas from the San Francisco airport. Besides, it was always a pleasure for the four of us to spend a few days together, before and after a trip. Bill Ford's friendship with Dick started during their freshman year in vet school. Dick was Bill's best man when he married Norma. Visiting them in the Bay Area was a special treat, yet I had a hollow feeling inside me, because I knew that this time, Dick wouldn't be with me. I had no premonition of what was to transpire within a week, not the faintest idea that Dick, who sat here beside me, would be dead in three months.

Finishing up Dick's back rub, I headed for the kitchen to get out the ingredients for our meal.

————

As I prepared dinner, I reflected on a phone conversation with my oldest daughter, months before I had solidified my plans for France.

"Sara, where does desire come from? Do you suppose it is in the genes...something you are born with?"

"Gosh, Mom, I don't know. You've been interested in French as long as I can remember."

"Well, I keep studying like it was important, as if there was something missing in me, an empty glass waiting to be filled or a blank canvas that needs to be painted. I'm seventy-five years old! What difference could it make? It seems so important, but it's almost like there is a necessity, something that I have to do now, or else…sort of an obsession! Why in the world would I go to so much trouble to try and learn more of the language at my age?" Pausing to reflect, "Actually, I feel like I am following in the footsteps of my mother. She loved Paris. When I think back, she took French lessons from a retired college professor when she was a little younger than what I am. Maybe I'm doing it for her, or even because of her. I've always felt that she was the one that gave me the 'travel bug.' Maybe it *is* in the genes. Maybe French has more of a meaning than I can imagine…"

"When you go to France, perhaps you'll find out. It should be a great experience whether you find all the answers. Remember, Mom, with all your kids, the practice, art and gardening, you somehow became a professional Belly Dancer. I remember when Dad drove you around on Saturday nights when you had gigs at different night clubs. Maybe it is the same thing. You wanted to become a dancer back then, and now you want to become an American who speaks French."

"I must admit that I have to accept your logic." We both laughed. Little did I know how this experience of travelling alone would give me confidence to travel later once I had lost Dick.

———

I had a French acquaintance, a teacher in Paris named Anne who had worked with me over the internet to help two students in Ethiopia. I had emailed Anne, explaining that I wanted to perfect my French and wondering if she knew anyone who could tolerate an American for a month. One of Anne's two sisters, Pascale, lived in Aix en Provence in Southern France with her husband, Guy, their son Vincent, and a little white dog, Tatine. Pascale seemed amenable—just the kind of situation I had wished for. I immediately began making plans.

"What do you think, Dick? Do you want me to go? Can you put up with me being gone for a month?" I found myself asking permission. After all, we had always been partners in everything we did so it was natural for each to ask the other for his or her opinion.

"Janet, it hasn't escaped my notice that you have been devouring French for ages. Of course I'll miss you, but this has been a dream of yours for a long time," Dick said magnanimously. "Stop thinking that there's something wrong with you. Lots of people go to countries to learn a foreign language. You've just had a lot of things on your plate. Now it looks like a good time to go."

I had given the time frame a lot of thought. The garden was nearing year's end. Dick was in good health. At seventy-eight, he might not be so healthy by the next year. And besides, I had always worked from the principle that if moments of opportunity were not seized, they might never come again.

Over the next several weeks, I made arrangements with Anne and Pascal. I checked with Bill and Norma Ford before buying a ticket from San Francisco to Paris, making sure I could stay at their house before my flight departed. Typically, the Fords would take us to the airport and pick us up on our return. Often we would drive down to the waterfront in San Francisco, where the cable cars start up the hill. There, we would find a seat in the crowded Buena Vista Bar and hoist an Irish coffee or two to make a toast for a great trip, and later, to celebrate a successful return. Next month, Dick planned to drive down to the Ford's house to meet me after I came off the plane. The Buena Vista tradition would top off my trip and a happy reunion with my beloved husband.

CHAPTER TWO
THE EXQUISITE DESIRE

In spite of my pre-trip anxieties, I felt empowered as I drove the rental car down through California. I clutched the steering wheel, as though holding the reins of my beautifully trained horse. With just a touch, the car leaped to obey. On the last stretch of Interstate 5, I glanced down at the speedometer to find I was going a shocking 100 miles per hour! I managed to get to the Ford's without a single mishap, obviously making good time. As I walked into their home, only my cramped hands reminded me of the stress and concentration required to get there. The trip to the airport the next day was also unbelievably flawless. With ease I found the car return building, caught the shuttle and entered the airport. Soon I was finding my seat on the nonstop flight to Paris. Managing to accomplish all of this without Dick was indeed stressful, but I was proud of myself. In spite of trepidations, I had solved many problems that I was unsure about. Because of my desire to speak a foreign language, I had mustered up the effort and had overcome my fear of failure.

————

Charles de Gaulle is a huge, but user friendly airport, and I quickly passed through customs. After a sleepless night, I rallied my logy body and dragged my favorite old duffle bag down two sets of escalators, watching for the signs to the TGV station, as Anne had instructed over email. She had arranged to leave school as soon as the lunch hour began and catch the metro to the airport. As I sat waiting for Anne, whom I'd never met in person, I zipped up my grey sweater against the wind, which steadily blew from the end of the building where the trains sat waiting for their departure time. Sleep would have felt good, but my anticipation outweighed my exhaustion.

Slowly, a warm feeling came over me as I tucked the collar of my sweater up to my chin. I could almost feel the warm embrace and sweet kiss Dick had given me as we said our goodbyes. He had such great kisses! I wished he was here with me, but what would he do while I sat in someone's house trying to speak French? At home, at least he would have our daughter, Laurie asking him to meet her for lunch or an evening movie.

While sitting there, I could feel a sense of accomplishment at getting to Paris alone, and yet also found myself anticipating my return to San Francisco when Dick would drive down, visit with the Fords and then be at the airport to greet me. I imagined rattling off some French while they admired my new-found vocabulary. Returning to the Ford's house, I would unpack a bottle of Gaillac wine, the kind Dick had raved about when he and I were in Southern France two years earlier. I would pull out some wonderful goat cheese and a baguette for all of us to share. I shivered with excitement just thinking how pleased Dick would be, knowing that I had brought back that special brand of French wine. Thinking of this scenario brought a smile to my face. It was even more worthwhile to take this trip alone, if only for the joy of greeting him after a month's separation.

A dark haired woman approached me, small and thin, dressed in dark colors, with a red scarf wrapped tightly around her neck. Kindness and gentleness seemed to express itself in her pretty face.

"Janet?" Anne questioned, with her eyes and voice.

"Yes. And you're Anne, right?" I remarked, somehow relieved to be greeted in English.

"We have a little time. We can go over there for some tea…or perhaps you are hungry?"

"Tea would be fine. I had breakfast on the plane."

"Then tea it is. I have your TGV ticket. I purchased a first class ticket over a month ago, so the price is much less. You will have more room and comfort for your trip. It will take about three and a half hours to get to where my sister lives."

After a cup of tea at the nearby coffee shop, we walked toward the trains.

"The voie for the train to Perpignon is six. Number 13 car will stop by the 'F' sign," Anne said, with quiet patience. "Now look up here and see where the platform signs give the letters. There's 'J,' so we'll just walk along here to 'F.'"

Quietly, the sleek silver train moved into the station. People on the platform waited as passengers stepped out. I was pleased to see that Voiture 13 was nearly in front of us. I gave Anne a hug and thanked her again. Soon, the almost silent bullet train left the switching yards and passed through the industrial section, picking up speed as it swooshed by the suburbs. The train moved so quickly that I couldn't catch the names of towns.

———

I stepped off the train into Southern France, following the crowd out of the station. Many of the passengers headed for parked cars while I stood in front of the station hoping someone would recognize me. Without Dick by my side, I felt quite vulnerable. We had traveled to many parts of the world, usually on the "cheap" which involved backpacking, sleeping on the floor or ground in little villages, or looking for the right time to catch the right train to a new destination. With Dick, travelling had always seemed so easy, so thrilling, and so enjoyable. Dick always referred to the two of us as "Hansel and Gretel." Whenever a problem came up, both of us worked to solve it like "well-oiled machines," another of Dick's favorite sayings. I was thankful that Anne had met me in Paris, making the next step on my journey effortless.

My unease dissipated as I watched a smiling blond woman, with a little white dog, approach.

"Janet! I am here! I am so glad you are waiting. I had traffic and was not here to greet you! This is Tatin." Pascale pointed to her little Jack Russell Terrier, took my bag and hugged me all at the same time.

At Pascale's home, days passed while I basked in the beautiful sunlight that delighted Van Gogh. Autumn weather made the days extremely pleasant. I climbed a hill near the apartment and painted Saint Victoire, the large mountain that is at the end of the Luberon, placing my paints on a limestone bench where Cezanne had arranged his oils on a pallet. He had painted the mountain several times, far more successfully than me. I wandered the landscape of Southern France loving the multiple rows of Cyprus and Pinion Pine. All the delightful-looking houses had the same ivory rectangle shape topped with red tile roofs and the Luberon mountain range served as a magnificent backdrop. Roman ruins, more common in Nimes and Orange, dotted the landscape. Each day seemed more glorious than the next as I saw and felt so much—my cup was full. The experiences surpassed all I had hoped for and expected.

When Pascale had an appointment, she dropped me off in the main section of Aix en Provence to spend a couple of hours looking around the town at shops and some of the old streets with many interesting buildings. I felt quite uneasy, sure I would get lost, since old European towns never seem to follow a grid. Streets end abruptly, and one angle is not the same as another. What should have carried me back to the boulevard only led me to another street, totally unfamiliar. I felt like a lost dog as my anxiety peaked, so I gave up exploring and lingered on the busy boulevard for a while, then walked up several blocks until I saw the Number One bus. Hoping it was going the right way, I felt greatly relieved when I recognized a crossroad just two blocks from Pascale and Guy's apartment. Sight-seeing alone was not very pleasant and hard for me to get used to.

The next day I changed my perspective. If I was going to be in Provence for a month, I would have to do much better. Even a dog uses his voice! Of course it was possible for me to ask French people where the boulevard was located if I got disoriented. I might have a little trouble understanding the rapid reply to my question, but the hand signals certainly helped. Soon the unsure feeling dissipated. I was determined to get the most out of this experience.

————

Guy had a program on his computer that gave me the opportunity to speak to Dick each day. On my second day in Provence, I made my first call and misjudged the time difference, awakening him at three in the morning. The following day, I did better.

"Hi hon, how is everything?"

"Oh, all right. I moved a bunch of those paving blocks that were in the driveway. I won't get started on my project this fall, but next spring I plan on adding to the walk below the last retaining wall. At least the blocks will be out of the way. There were more there than I thought. How's your trip coming along? Are you learning any new French words that say 'I love you' or 'How about a little sex before the fromage?' You know I miss you."

I giggled like a schoolgirl. The two of us often carried on with sexy banter—pretty spicy for an old married couple. I couldn't think of any appropriate comment with Guy standing nearby (who might just understand a little off-color English) but I was also anxious to tell him about my first couple of days that seemed to just zip by: the glorious weather, the delicious landscape, and the huge assortment of cheese and wine at the market. I told him I was going to bring him my favorite cheese so he could try some of it. As for French, I expressed my delight, thinking I was already learning quite a bit. Everyone was so patient and such great people to be around. I really didn't miss Dick. After all, it had only been a few days. I was having a wonderful time. Sometimes, I couldn't believe it…that I was actually here!

I did have some misgivings, living in a stranger's house as a guest, something that I had never done before. Pascale was very involved with her daughters and sister as well as her elderly mother. Before the week was out, I began to feel that I was not doing enough. I offered money for groceries, but the supermarche, a French word for all super markets, required a special card instead of cash. I tried to be helpful, washing the dishes, setting the table and preparing a meal. To give Pascale some time to herself, I walked Tatine, painted, or hiked to places where the view was especially nice. Whatever problems that may have arisen during my month-long stay would be left unresolved, because my dream ended abruptly. I stayed with Pascale and Guy for only seven days

————

Unbeknownst to me, about an hour after speaking to Dick, he was at the computer, when suddenly he was consumed with a deep strong pain in his chest. He called 911 and drove the car to the bottom of the hill to wait for the ambulance. By nightfall, it became apparent that he had suffered a dissected aorta. If one layer of his aorta hadn't held, he would have had an aneurism. The consequence of this dissection caused a balloon of blood which blocked off one of his femoral arteries and put his kidneys at risk. Doctors performed emergency surgery to save his leg and he felt much better the following day. Having never spent one night in a hospital in his entire life, he believed he would only be there for a day or two. Feeling strong and confident, he told Laurie not to call me and ruin my long-desired dream.

Yet, she called anyway at ten-thirty at night. I was asleep when Guy entered the bedroom to tell me that Laurie was on the phone. Prior to my trip, I had contemplated the possibility of Dick having a health problem, and just in case, had taken a course in CPR. I even tried to imagine what it would be like to be alone in the house. Yet, I felt confident that such a moment was in the distant future.

After the call, I had mixed emotions and felt incredibly guilty. I didn't want to leave France. For years, I had wanted to come and speak French. This opportunity was so delicious, so wonderful. I believed that Dick would be fine in a few days, that his health problem just couldn't be that serious. France seemed so important to me. I accepted that I would have to go home, but I attempted to make arrangements with great reluctance.

The next day was another beauty. Gazing out the window at a scene that could have been a postcard, I placed a call to Dick at the hospital. He sounded quite normal, yet was clearly disappointed to hear from me.

"So the bird let the cat out of the bag," referring to Laurie's nickname, "Little Bird." "Well, I'm sorry. I hoped that you wouldn't have to know, but I guess there's nothing I can do about it. The surgery went OK. For a while last night, I thought I was going to lose my leg. The pain was really terrific. Now it feels fine, and no pain, but I can't get out of bed yet. When I first had the pain in my chest, I thought I was having a heart attack. Well, that's it for now. They want to take my blood pressure. Bye." Typically, Dick did not want to linger with a difficult conversation, so I felt secretly pleased that he seemed his normal self.

My airline ticket, dated November 1, posed a dilemma: how was I going to arrange to get home? Laurie, the "go-to" girl, the one that everyone called upon to solve computer and travel problems, the one who constantly got stressed out, who worried about every problem of her friends and family, and still managed to make 'A's' in college, took the initiative to solve my problem. She arranged for a new flight reservation, not only from Paris, but from San Francisco to Medford. Three days after Dick's sudden illness, I left for Paris. Before leaving, I rushed through the supermarche, purchasing several varieties of cheese and a baguette, but forgot the Gaillac wine.

Pascale helped out by buying the TGV ticket to Charles de Gaulle Airport. Dropping me off at the station, she expressed her sadness, "Janet, you must come back to us! We so hope that

Dick will be fine. All our love to you! Bisous, bisous, bisous!" Her French words for kisses remained with me for the whole trip home. She gave me a tight hug, her eyes filling with tears. I hugged back, wanting to cry, but this all seemed so unreal. I felt rushed, pushed into something I didn't want, hadn't anticipated, and didn't believe was really happening.

I stepped off the train at the airport to find Anne waiting for me. The following day, I gratefully let Anne resolve the many problems we encountered at the airport. She rushed from one place to another, searching for someone who would know what to do. I suspected that with my limited ability to rapidly converse in French, I would still be in some line as the plane left for America. Thanks to Anne, I finally paid for my ticket and she escorted me toward the gate as we said our goodbyes. Questions raced through my head as I sat alone at the gate. Would I ever return to France? Would there ever be another chance to immerse myself in the French language? How stupid to even care! It was Dick I should be thinking about, yet I expected him to be well by the time I arrived at his bedside.

CHAPTER THREE
THE BEGINNING OF THE END

When the plane arrived in San Francisco, the Fords were waiting with hugs, but no smiles. We solemnly drove back to their house. Because it was nearly ten when the plane landed, we didn't get to bed until after midnight. The five a.m. alarm the next morning startled me awake, and Bill and Norma drove me back to the airport in the dark. They quickly placed my luggage on a cart for me.

"Golly, Janet. We really don't know what to say. We hope Dick will be better and we can see you guys soon. It's so hard to think of Dick in a hospital bed!" Bill suddenly smiled, "I'll bet he's working on the tough Sunday crossword puzzle." His comment and smile relieved some of my tension as I trudged back into the airport.

My neighbors picked me up in Medford and took me directly to the hospital. I walked in to see my five worried children and several grandchildren huddled in the waiting room. Seeing so many of my offspring, my first thought was to immediately prepare myself for the job of producing meals for everyone. It seemed so strange, with everyone shifting uneasily, to feel the anxiety in the room. Each of them would prefer to be with Dick, rather than in the waiting room, but only two at a time could be with him. The gravity of the situation—why they were all there—didn't seem to reach me. I gave each one of them a hug and a kiss before heading down the hall to his room, unsure of what to expect.

When I walked into the room, Dick's smile, his voice and his confidence eased my mind. He didn't even look sick. What seemed out of place was that his clothing and everything on his bed was white. Dick usually was dressed in colorful T-shirts. He had been moved from CCI to a regular room for heart patients. The bed was elevated with all sorts of lines running to and from places on his body keeping us from having any kind of real hug. I gave up any thought of sharing the day-old baguette and goat cheese that were still in my backpack. With nurses coming and going, and my children taking turns visiting, the room seemed overly crowded. The atmosphere of chaos separated the two of us and I couldn't feel the connection I wanted with him—even touching his hand seemed difficult and unsatisfying. The quick smile he had given me didn't last long. Something was bothering him.

"No recriminations" he said, obviously seeing the frown on my face. Perhaps I looked that way from two days with little sleep as I traveled nearly half way around the world. But Dick no doubt was remembering my heartfelt advice that he often resisted—all the times I had encouraged exercise and a restricted diet. He probably anticipated a lambasting. In his mind he could hear me saying, "You bastard! I told you this would happen! I tried to get you to exercise more, lay off the high cholesterol diet you ate when I wasn't around. I tried to get you to see the doctor more often and get your blood pressure checked, to see if you should be on a higher dose. I warned you not to sit and watch hours of television. This is your own fault!"

"No recriminations" I knew what those two words meant and I knew why he had said them. I chose not to say anything to him because I knew him so well. I realized what he thought each time I was in his presence, those unspoken words, blaming him for his problems. I even regretted that I had made such a point about his diet, lack of exercise and the hours in front of the television. In a way, my past efforts to keep him healthy, the efforts that he often chose to ignore, were separating us at this moment as much as all the tubes and monitors.

He never seemed happy to see me, even grouchy, which surprised Sara and Hal, our two children who most often came to his room.

———

The immediate crisis seemed to pass during the following week. Work and school drew several family members back to their homes. Laurie, who lived locally, struggled to maintain her scholastic standing and concentrate on college, while trying to support Dick and me. Dick continued to battle the odds of very elevated blood pressure and a severe lack of appetite. I had difficulty understanding what the doctors told me—either their words were unclear, or I failed to listen. The twelve inch dissected aorta was causing the blood to fill the enlarged ballooned sack that was gauzy thin. It was the only thing that had kept him from an aneurism causing immediate death. However, this ballooning also caused his heart to beat fast and raised his blood pressure, yet not enough blood was going to his kidneys.

Dick became unhappy with Laurie as well as me. The two of us worried too much, trying to "fix" things. Laurie constantly straightened his room and spent hours on the internet looking for special foods that would reverse his loss of appetite. She was like a bee in the room, searching for a way out, not for herself but for her dad.

In contrast to the frenzied activities of Laurie and me, Sara and Hal had an easier time just being with Dick to keep him company and help in little ways. They worked out a twenty-four hour program for spending time with Dick. At times, Hal would sleep on the floor, or sacked out on the waiting room sofa, his six-foot, two-inch frame hanging off of it. Sara, a veterinarian, wanted to be in Dick's room when the doctors made their rounds early in the morning. As we watched Dick decline, both of them looked nearly as bad from their round-the-clock vigil.

I couldn't stand the pressure, preferring to fuss at home while my kids took turns with Dick. I didn't want to see the negative changes in his condition. I cooked for those who stayed at the house and spent nights trying to think of foods that Dick could eat and would like. I constantly searched for answers that the heart and kidney doctors might have missed. One day, I made him rice to help cure the diarrhea caused by his medication, but he only took a few bites, then pushed it away. Another time, he asked for a tri-tip beef steak, so I carefully cut the cooked meat into narrow strips, included a small baked potato and wrapped the meal in a towel to keep it hot. He swallowed only two small pieces and was done.

I found some relief from my distress when I rode Hussy; only on my mare's back was I able to stop thinking of saving someone I couldn't save. Later I realized Hussy had kept me from having a nervous breakdown. My life had become a nightmare, and I was barely keeping my head above water when things worsened.

As the doctor had feared, the ballooning aorta caused Dick's kidneys to fail. Moments of hope that he would return home began to fade. Gone were those heady days soon after my arrival from France, where he had used a walker to plod down the hall. I shudder now at the memory of getting up at five in the morning to take him for his first dialysis when he was temporarily placed in a nursing facility across from the hospital. A husky nurse had placed him in my car. I drove to the Dialysis Center, went around the car, and tried to get Dick into a wheelchair. But he couldn't stand and I couldn't hold him. He sank to the curb as I frantically ran inside for help. It seemed to me that this was all happening to someone else, not my beloved husband.

After he was returned to the hospital, an extra bed was brought in for the family members who insisted on remaining with him constantly. Dan sent his son, Andrew, who spent over a month, staying most of the time at the hospital with his grand-dad. Sara came and went several times from Wisconsin. When Andrew left, Dan's daughter, Cassandra came for a month, during her college Christmas break. Dick was losing several pounds a day. When his weight dropped to one hundred and sixty pounds, he actually looked great to me. He was at a weight that fit his frame, but he would only eat a little ice cream and that was all. Days later, he began to look like a prisoner from a Nazi concentration camp. Sara and I argued and cajoled, but Dick refused to eat, roaring, "Everything tastes like shit!"

With all the help from family and all the stress, I never felt like there was even a moment for intimacy. And I could not see clearly enough to try to create it. I felt terribly cheated. There were always tubes and monitors on his arms or chest and a catheter to his bladder. How was it possible to give the hugs and kisses that I wanted to give him? I longed for some sort of closure, some feeling of being close to him, to his body, his touch, his kisses. There didn't even seem to be a time where we could tell each other of our undying love. Perhaps it was because there were always other people in the room. I didn't realize this until after he died. Neither of us totally recognized that there was a possibility of death. Both of us assumed that a reversal in his condition was just around the corner. We had watched the years go by, yet we hadn't considered death. No one truly can. I had never thought of Dick as an old man, even though his hair and beard were white, and he no longer had the vigor I expected. Eight months earlier, we had traveled to Southern India for a month. Dick was full of enthusiasm and enjoyed the food and customs of the country. He survived the thirty-six hours of flight time back to the states with no ill effect. Yet here I was now, looking at a sack containing his dark-looking urine, with only a paucity of the volume required. Once he got put on dialysis, vital tubes connected near his neck, and later at his groin. Then the dreaded MRSA signaled that the end was near. Now, he was not only dying, but must be handled with gloves and gowns. My heart cried out in agony for my "real" husband.

On a sunny pleasant morning, a few days before Christmas, the ambulance brought Dick home to die. I cooked for Sara, Hal and Cassandra and walked in and out of the living room, where the hospital bed had been placed. I got up frequently in the night to find one of the three rubbing Dick's head or part of his back. I had to ask myself why I wasn't by his side as they were. I felt completely shattered, so full of frustration and incredible sadness, unable to solve the problem of making Dick well. I had tried to find answers where there were none, and so I couldn't stand to simply *be* with him or watch him decline. There are no words that can describe my mental state which caused me to continually separate myself from a person that I treasured so much. I couldn't really believe the magnitude of the situation even though the tragedy was taking place before my eyes. The reality was that subconsciously I expected each time I returned to him, I would find that he was getting better. I was blessed or cursed with incredible optimism; thus each time I came to his bedside, it was even more of a severe blow to my psyche.

Christmas day arrived with bright sunlight after a night of light rain.

"Boppie has given us the best Christmas present," Cassandra said softly, using the name all of Richard's grandchildren called him. As I looked at this lovely young lady, I thought that perhaps I should be happy instead of sad. Dick and I had produced five wonderful children and they, in turn, had produced eleven loving, caring grandchildren. He would be alive as long as they and their children continued to live. He would continue to be part of who they are. While I hoped this thought would help me, there really wasn't any way to find help, hope or words and thoughts that comforted me on this journey of death and loss.

On the twenty-sixth of December, Dick took his last breath as I stood watching. He had been sleeping restlessly for three days. As fate would have it, the two of us were finally alone. For the last several weeks I had watched his body use itself up. All of his protein requirements were utilized by depleting his muscles. The water which makes up most of the body was nearly gone. He hadn't drunk any to speak of, no more than just a sip or two. All that was left was that strong heart that I used to listen to when I laid my head against his chest. The wonderful and only man in my life had slowly vanished before my eyes. He was, in the end, unrecognizable. *I knew he was dying but I couldn't believe or comprehend it.* With his last breath, the love and joy of my life was no more. I just stood and watched and watched. I felt as if in a void, a cloud of nothing. I knelt on the floor beside his bed and took his still warm hand into mine.

As I held it, I recalled that Dick had been an undying fan of the television series called "Lonesome Dove." He had added a phrase from it to his own lexicon. "It's been quite a party." I believe that if Dick's death had been anything like a movie, this is what he would have said just minutes before his passing.

"Yes, it's been quite a party. Good-bye sweet love," I whispered softly into his wonderful hand, the hand that he used to place around my waist, the hand I held when we danced, the hand that put a gold wedding ring on my finger fifty-five and a half years ago. My "Hansel" who had joined me in life's great adventures. In that hand, I placed my last kiss and closed his fingers over it.

PART TWO

Depression…Heartbreak…Denial…New decisions…
New directions…Self discovery

CHAPTER FOUR
THE AFTERMATH

I found that crying came very easily and I did it a lot. When I was alone, I tried to wail, but usually, I was so quiet that no one would have noticed. I remembered the last moments vividly, as I looked for the last time at my sweet Dickie, while a man and woman lifted him onto a gurney covered with a black bag. I turned my back on the unbearable sight of him being taken away from me forever. The sound of the zipper closing the bag was the most horrible sound I would ever hear.

I arranged for the cremation. Going alone into the post office to pick up the registered box that contained his ashes was nearly more than I could stand. Signing for it upset me even more. Finally reaching the car, I cried over the steering wheel, unable to drive, filled with remorse. Over and over, the "finalizing" continued to take place.

We held the memorial service at the Unitarian Fellowship in Ashland. Neighbors and friends helped prepare the food. I placed Dick's Kufi cap from Uzbekistan—the one he wore everyday, all day, except when he slept—on the top step at the front of the church. I walked to the podium and looked at the small group, perhaps thirty, which didn't seem like enough. Shouldn't there be thousands of people? Of our children, only Laurie and Hal were present. Yet we would have another service in Wisconsin during the coming summer for the rest of our friends and family.

"For this occasion," I couldn't believe how strongly I was able to speak, "I wanted to tell you what I thought were the most important attributes of this man who had occupied so much of my life. First was his ability to take in knowledge like a magnet draws iron filings." I continued to speak for several minutes. I was so anxious for all to know the wonderful and unusual man whom I had loved.

"Where most of us are content to say that we heard or read it, Dick was able to be much more precise. He could tell you what year a war started and what precipitated it and by whom. He could give you names and dates. For many who knew him for a short period of time during our many travels, their most lasting memory of him would be of his many stories. Full of pain and pathos, he would act them out as his listeners laughed with tears rolling down their cheeks. Two of the best were his two weeks in the Cheyenne City Jail and the time he separated his ribs wrestling in college."

I mentioned many things that I felt were important, vignettes about his life, our travels, his love for his children and grandchildren. There seemed to be so much more that I wanted to add, so much more of the full life he had led.

"Those that knew you and those that loved you, we will all miss talking with you, learning from you and enjoying your wonderful company."

I looked at my tall handsome son, Hal, and saw him crying for the first time since he was a small child. He, Sara and Laurie had consistently given their father back all the love he had given them throughout his illness. Without them, I would never have made it through such a long and difficult time.

I thought that mourning would not take long, not realizing that it really hadn't begun. There was still the thought that Dick would come in the door or be with me in bed. I had a dream the night after Dick died.

"What are you doing here?" I said. Dick looked pale.

"I'll be with you always." He replied.

I told my children and friends about it. They all thought I was very lucky to have Dick say that to me. "I guess so. Yes, I suppose so." It wasn't much solace, but it was all I was going to get. In the future, it would mean much more to me. Even then, I suspected this.

———

To assuage my grief, I began to redefine my life. First, I changed the location of our...my bed, hoping that rearranging furniture would cure some of the sorrow when I climbed into it I then cancelled the cable service as the television would no longer be part of my life. Eating in restaurants and buying ice cream, both things that Dick loved to do, were now an anathema. I began to read the myriad of books that Dick had gathered over the years. It would take me another lifetime to read them all. My activities of hiking, skiing, dog training and horse riding continued. I felt so lucky that I had these as I strained to fill the day, to be so tired that I would quickly fall asleep. Still the pillow was often wet with tears.

I vowed to ask neighbors and Oliver (the high school boy who watched over dogs and garden while I was away) for more help with difficult projects. The paving bricks were first on the agenda.

Dick had placed them near the strawberry bed. It took Oliver two and a half hours, using the wheelbarrow, to put them in the back of the pickup truck. I planned on taking them back to Cascade Block for a refund. When I saw how long it took Oliver to load and unload them, it didn't surprise me that Dick could have caused his aorta to split with this spurt of heavy duty activity.

"You're a tough broad," one of Dick's childhood friends said to me. "You'll be just fine." Those words echoed in my head as I began solving problems that Dick had taken care of in the past, such as sorting the mail and paying the credit card and utility bills. Laurie patiently explained how to pay online. It took several months for me to feel comfortable with the added book work and the checking account. I fretted that I would forget to pay a bill on time, usually thinking about it in the middle of the night. I had this uneasy feeling when I purchased something from the hardware store that it wasn't the right product, not the one that Dick would need or choose to fix a problem. It was so hard to take over his jobs. As for the tools! Getting used to them was even more challenging.

I felt like my days were empty, void, wasted. No matter how I filled them, they did not fulfill me. Songs entered my consciousness, sometimes during the night. This went on for months. Mostly, they were songs from the forties, during World War II. Those that lingered were: "I don't want to walk without you, Baby"; "I'll walk alone"; "Stardust"; "Nevertheless"; "I'll be seeing you in all the old familiar places..."; and "It's too late now to forget your smile, the way I cling when we dance awhile. Too late now to forget and go on to someone new..."

"How am I ever going to get over wanting you and missing you?" I screamed to him in our now empty house.

CHAPTER FIVE
IN SEARCH OF HOPEFULLNESS: THE ODESSEY

I continued to invite friends for dinner, perhaps more than I had before Dick's death. Machtild and her husband, Arthur, came for poached salmon one mid-winter evening. Machtild was one of my hiking buddies. Born in Germany, she had met Arthur in South Africa. During the meal, she extolled the virtues of South Africa and the Ocovongo Delta, where the two of them had spent some of their courting days. I looked up tours to South Africa later that evening, desperate to have something to look forward to. Travel, which I always loved, seemed the answer. My solo trip to France, even though cut short, had given me the confidence to get back into an adventure. Nomad Tours popped up on the screen. There was a tour in April for three weeks beginning in Cape Town and ending at Victoria Falls via Namibia, Botswana and Zimbabwe. It was a camping tour with tents. I contacted the tour company but faced obvious reluctance to booking an unknown woman with a birth date of 1932.

"Perhaps you would be happier with an accommodated tour?"

the email diplomatically replied to my inquiry. But I didn't want a "mushy" tour. I wanted it to be hard and somewhat uncomfortable, one that traveled deeper into the country—a trip that would keep my mind off of my debilitating grief. I wanted to be with adventurous young people who didn't care if I was married, widowed or had five kids and eleven grandchildren. Realizing the tour company's hesitation, I came up with a solution. Feeling that I owed Hal a great deal for being so patient and helpful with his father, I hatched an idea to thank him for all he had done for me, before and after Dick's death. He had stayed for an extra month, accomplishing a number of tasks that Dick had left unfinished. Just his presence made me feel better. I thought it would be wonderful to share Africa with him. To my delight, he agreed.

The tour company asked me to fax a letter from my doctor, assuring them that I was fit enough to be included on the trip. As I waited at the Medford Health Center, I noticed many elderly people. Some were in wheelchairs, others with a walker, many with caregivers accompanying them. My thoughts drifted to "what ifs" about Dick. "Is this what I would want for Dick? If he had recovered enough to leave the hospital, would he have been the same as he was before, just watching television and refusing to exercise…or being unable to do it? If his kidneys were only semi-functional, what would I have had to change in the way I cooked? Would he have been happy to eat his food without salt? Could I have left him alone as I had in the past, while I hiked the mountains or rode my horse?" I sadly mulled the possibilities and reluctantly concluded he had departed this earth at the right time for him, and perhaps for me, too. Every time I saw an old person struggling across a street or being wheeled along at the supermarket, I tried to rationalize Dick's death. Still, it didn't help me for very long. The unbelievable sadness refused to fade. I had made progress, but it seemed incremental, at best.

————

Hal and I began our adventure with a drive to the Ford's house while I navigated. After we arrived at the Fords, the four of us had a pleasant day as Norma and Bill became better acquainted with Hal. Together, we drove to San Francisco, down by the bay, where the cable cars start up the hill. We sat in the familiar surroundings of the Buena Vista Bar that Dick loved when he and I left or returned from our overseas trips. I ordered the usual. When the waitress arrived with the four glasses filled with whiskey and coffee, topped with whipped cream, I proposed a toast to Richard. All did their best not to cry, but the napkins under the Irish Coffee glasses soon found their way to our eyes.

The next day, Hal and I left for Frankfurt. By the time we reached Cape Town, over twenty four hours had passed. After arriving at five in the morning, it took an hour to retrieve luggage and pass immigration. Once Hal and I were in our hotel room, we collapsed onto the beds, not rising until the following morning.

We spent two days seeing the highlights of Cape Town. "Dick would have loved to see this city," I thought. We very much opposed Apartheid. "I think he would be pleased with the changes. It's not perfect, but it is sure an improvement over the past." The excitement of the trip, the new country, and different faces were a welcome relief. What a blessing not to be mired in depression!

The next morning, rain pelted us as all members of the tour group assembled. The rain diminished as we hurriedly climbed aboard the white truck. Our African adventure had begun. I recalled what Bill Ford had said when I told him about my plans for the trip. "Have you done any research on this organization? It could be one of these scams, or some lousy outfit that just dumps you in God-forsaken places. There are all those diseases besides malaria. You should have gone for the accommodated. You're no spring chicken!"

"No, Bill. I just took a chance. Most things work out OK. I've paid the money and I'll put up with whatever happens." Those words echoed in my head as we drove to our first stop for the night. I grinned as Hal and I struggled to put up the tent that first day. It didn't take me long to realize that most of my friends would not have enjoyed sleeping on the ground for three weeks or putting up this heavy canvas tent each evening. Hal didn't seem to mind and neither did I since I desperately needed every moment of hardship to take my mind off of grief.

Once the tents were up, and in spite of the gray sky and lingering wetness, the tour guides introduced us to a small man, a descendent of the San people. With his two front teeth missing, strange-sounding words came out as he struggled with English. He led us into the mountainous area behind the camp site. Others didn't seem to be as interested as me in his knowledge and descriptions. I could have spent days trailing behind this man, who showed us ancient rock art, explaining the secrets of people who know every insect, snake and leaf. Still I really missed Dick, always wondering what he would have thought about the truck, the tour, the scenery and later, the African tribes our group encountered.

That first night, I lay down in our tent and tucked myself into the sleeping bag. Without a thought, I was asleep.

Word passed quickly about my age. Several of them expressed shock, since I had little trouble keeping up with all the activities. I took my turn in the food preparation and cleanup. No one seemed to care if I was married or how many children I had. I made no mention of my widowhood.

Hal liked helping Boniswa, the cook. If she needed to move something heavy, he was there to lift it for her. Occasionally, a young Korean came to help me with the tent, since Hal kept busy helping Boniswa. I thought of Dick as I proudly watched Hal. Dick had always tried to be helpful, too—part of what had won my heart so long ago.

Within days, the group of twenty-four began to meld. We made a decision for all to change seating, moving one seat up in the truck each morning, so everyone could have the 'pleasure' of riding at the back, especially when the road was full of holes and bumps. Lockers at the rear went from the floor to the ceiling, one for each person. Hal chose the most difficult one to reach. He managed to fix the windows so they could be opened half way, and folded pieces of cardboard to keep them from chattering. When the truck got stuck in very deep sand, it was Hal who sat under the truck with a jack, humming as he slowly lifted the axle, while several cute young girls stuffed rocks under the rear wheels. They weren't alone. All of us were like ants, running along the dry river bed, carrying rocks to make a road for the truck to back onto. Our guide and driver, Joe, tried to go forward several times. Hal, like his father, was extremely diplomatic, trying to assure and encourage Joe, knowing that the only way to extricate the truck was to go in reverse. From experience, he realized what was possible and what worked. Joe knew that going forward hadn't worked but he didn't think going in reverse would be any better. Reluctantly, he decided to try. When it came time to push, all of us found a spot on the front and sides, grabbing any part of the truck that was available. Joe nervously shoved the gear into reverse and slowly released the clutch. We all began to scream in unison as we pushed with all our might. The rear wheels grabbed the stones and started to move over the other rocks placed behind the truck. Our screaming increased in volume! When the truck hit the solid footing of the road, we all rushed to hug each other. What a moment! Perhaps a highlight of the trip. Bill Ford's cautioning words echoed in my head once again, and yet, here we were, working through the obstacles as they arose.

Sleep came easily on this trip. "Rise and shine" usually took place before sunrise. One early morning, in Namibia, our group climbed the red and apricot colored dunes, the world's highest. Damp with sweat in the cold air, we laughed and played on top, as the sun rose. Even then, my thoughts were of Dick. I tried my best to forget his last days. Instead I focused on wishing he were part of this adventure. He would savor the best moments and the worst, ready to retell them to his many friends in the future.

Three weeks passed quickly with every day full of new experiences of African geography. There was a morning canoe trip on the Orange River. Later we stood above the second largest canyon to the American Grand Canyon. The Fish River, much like the Colorado, echoed far below the pink and golden walls.

On the Atlantic coast, we visited Swakopmud where the frigid waters come straight from Antarctica. In Botswanna, we camped beside the Spitzkoff Mountains which are enormous smooth boulders that tower over the desert. All of us climbed up one section for a view. We took lots of pictures at the Tropic of Capricorn, and our big white truck stopped for us to marvel at the enormous trunks of the Baobob trees. Springbok, zebras and termite nests became commonplace. We viewed elephants, giraffes, hippos and rhinos, watched herds of antelope and groups of Orynx. We spent two nights in the Okovongo Delta. An elephant walked beside our tent one night while we camped with the local tribe. Earlier we had listened to them sing by the campfire. African voices are so unique. The sound, language, music and harmony are mesmerizing yet one man's voice reminded me of Dick's singing.

Each part of the day seemed to have a highlight. Our final destination was Zimbabwe where we witnessed magnificent Victoria Falls! No one took pictures since the spray totally drenched our giddy group. I stood viewing this incredible scene, soaked to the skin, wishing Dick could see what I saw. As he had spoken to me in my dream, it occurred to me that maybe he was here, "with me always."

When the tour ended, Hal and I reluctantly bid farewell to the group. We took a plane back to Cape Town where we spent a few days with Coral and Jack, friends of Machtild's, she who had aroused my desire to travel to South Africa. I continued to view Cape Town as Dick might—listening to the problems and issues as he would have. Yet, I felt unequal to the task. Dick would have known the history, the variety of languages and all the tribes.

Our trip back to Oregon took several days. Soon it was time for Hal to return to his home in Wisconsin. I drove him to the airport. As he lifted out his luggage, I gazed at my tall son. He was such a handsome man. The African tan seemed to highlight his blue eyes.

"I really can't tell you what I enjoyed the most. We had a wonderful time. Lots of memories. Mom, I love you!" He gave me a tight hug which I returned as I laid my head on his shoulder. Then I stepped back to wave goodbye.

"Have a safe flight. I'll call you in a day or so. Say hello to Chelsea for me. I imagine that she'll want to know everything her dad saw."

CHAPTER SIX
THE MEMORIAL

As I drove back to my home on the hill, spring was everywhere. The sweet smell of blossoming manzanita filled the air. The scrub oaks were producing baby green leaves. Apparently a neighbor had just mowed his lawn, as the fresh cut smell filled my car. Daffodils greeted me as I pulled in the drive.

I went to my bedroom to change from the sweatshirt that had solved the morning chill, putting on a t-shirt instead. I glanced to my left where Dick's ashes were contained in a wooden box. My gaze wandered above it to a picture of us when we were in our twenties. By then, we had four children. I picked up the picture, planning to wipe away any dust that had collected. In the photo, I was sitting on his lap as he smiled up at me with such a look of pleasure. I looked at my expression to see that little sexy smile that only Dick would understand.

I set the picture down as the terrible feeling inside of me suddenly returned. "How could you leave me like this? I warned you! I begged you! Take care of yourself! Do it for me!" I wailed into the silence, sobbing as I held my head with both hands, then

I sat on the bed looking at the picture again. Tears clouded my vision and dropped into my lap. I reflected on how wonderful Africa had been. I had loved every minute, loved being with Hal, enjoyed the young happy group, loved it all…but it was not going to be that easy to move forward. Dick was not coming back, nor was he going away. He often appeared in my dreams. I wiped tears as I hiked, blubbered as I weeded the garden, lamented as I drove the car. I missed him when I wanted to share a movie or an article in the paper. The crossword puzzles in the daily paper would never get filled again by his pen. I would have to learn to be alone, without him, without his love, without his touch, his voice.

That night, he appeared in my dream again. He was standing, facing away from the doorway. I held him as tightly as I could. "Don't leave me! Don't leave me! Don't leave me!" I screamed, but he slumped in my arms and was gone.

———

The spring months hurried by, however I was not looking forward to the first week in June when I needed to travel to Wisconsin. I would love seeing all my children, grandchildren and many of my friends, but I wasn't anxious to participate in another memorial for Richard. I feared it would just reopen the deep sadness that I had tried so hard to dispel. I suspected that Sara would have problems too. She had made such a huge effort to solve Dick's medical problems, being with him, by his bedside, for days and weeks until the end.

A large group turned out for the Memorial Service, including Dick's brother, cousins and other friends from his teenage years, and friends of our children who had known him since the time when they were small children. Our grandson, Sean, born the same month as cousins, Cassandra and Chelsea, rose to speak. He had just entered his last year of pre-med—our daughter, Sheila's, brilliant and funny son.

"Boppie will be like a kind of jelly fish, one that never dies because it can reproduce itself without benefit of sex. It just changes from one form to another." He paused, waiting for a reaction. He searched the crowd for a little smile or smirk, realizing quickly that his light humor hadn't reached anyone. "Well, like a jelly fish..." Sean tried again, emphasizing each word, not sure at all that anyone understood him. "In this case with his children and grandchildren, just changing forms." Many might not remember such an unusual remark, yet it brought a smile to my face every time I thought of it.

Several members of the family rose to express their pleasure at having been part of Dick's life. Sara had a very hard time, stopping several times to compose herself. Sheila, Hal's twin, had a long list of adjectives describing her Dad's special qualities. Two sons-in-law rose to speak, each holding back sobs. Other friends stepped forward to tell the large group what Dick had meant to them and spoke about their common history. Soon, it was my turn. I could not believe that it was possible for me to stand in front of this gathering. When I saw Meryl Streep speak at her lover's funeral in the movie, 'Out of Africa', at the time, I thought it would be impossible for Meryl's character to be so sad and yet capable of controlling her emotions. Now it was my turn. I, too, felt as if I were an actress, just speaking words. This didn't seem like a funeral, just a gathering of friends and family. Months had passed. The location seemed so distant from my living room where I watched Dick take his last breath. It seemed easier to talk about Dick and the life the two of us had shared while here in Wisconsin.

"It is difficult to realize that this wonderful man who had so fulfilled my life and had such a loving and profound effect on his family and friends is gone. All had such hopes that there would be a reversal of his medical problems." I spoke of friends calling from Bulgaria and France, e-mails from England, his brother from Chicago, his cousins from Pennsylvania and Kansas City, his classmates from California and Arizona, his childhood friends from Arkansas, Medford and Colorado, many friends from Wisconsin and Oregon. I mentioned how blessed Dick was to have so many people who he cared about and who cared about him. I talked about his life, his love for adventure, history, politics and above all, his family. I was amazed that I spoke for so long and managed so well. Finally, I finished by saying, "Our Boppie died on December twenty-sixth. His beloved Sara and Hal, who had done so much to keep him alive and comfortable, were at his side. His grand-daughter, Cassandra, nick-named 'Sweetie Bumpskin,' and I completed the circle."

Dan's oldest was the first grandchild to marry, a week after the memorial. At the beginning of the service, the minister mentioned Boppie's absence. The tears started to fill my eyes, but I managed to stop the flow. In some countries it might be all right to break into sobs that within me were terribly close, to allow myself to fall to my knees in inconsolable wails. But this is America where grief is expected to be covered with a stiff upper lip.

Two days later, I returned to Oregon.

CHAPTER SEVEN
FRENCH WITH A VENGENCE

I have always relished the summer months in Southern Oregon with long days and profuse flowers. I could expect lots of sunny weather and this year, I shared time with three of Dan's children who each came individually. Andrew arrived first, and Lindsay, Laurie's oldest daughter arrived near the end of his visit. They were soul mates, born within a month of each other, twenty three years earlier. Alex, the youngest, who loved horses and theater, arrived next. Cassandra, now twenty one, came last. She had taken a week off from summer work to see me. I admit, I felt the best when I had company, but sometimes even worse when they left. After her college finals, Laurie had gone to Wisconsin for the memorial service and was away for the rest of the summer. With the house empty, I resumed my French studies without understanding why. Concentrating on nouns and verbs did fill up the long evenings.

Sadness returned with a vengeance near the end of August on Richard's birthday. My own birthday in July didn't seem to bother me much. I had often thrown parties to surprise Dick starting when we were living in Vet Village in Ft. Collins, before Sara was born. Everywhere I went, everywhere I looked, I thought of Dick. I found some solace when riding Hussy on a mountain trail, with my neighbor and her horse. Ferociously doing an hour's worth of laps in the pool was a temporary cure. Hiking a steep trail with friends seemed a plus…until I returned home.

The desire to return to France took hold of me, this time, more insistent than before. It seemed necessary to leave on October first, as I had done the year before. Unfortunately, my friends from Aix en Provence could not accommodate me, because Pascale and Anne's mother was quite ill.

"Maybe I should just get a Frequent Flyer ticket and go to Paris, then figure out where to go and what to do," I said to Sara.

"Mom, that doesn't make any sense and you know it. Besides, you don't want to just be in a hotel room, saying 'hello,' 'goodbye,' 'thank you,' and ordering a 'café crème.' You want to speak heavy duty French. Maybe a language program would work."

Off the phone, Sara started looking for answers on the internet. "There must be something available that would suit Mom," she likely said to herself. I got an email soon after. "Here's a couple of sites that you might check out. It's mostly semesters abroad and stuff like that, but you may see something that seems to fit what you are looking for."

I felt extremely thankful that I have a batch of children who care about me. I guess it's what parents hope for when they are changing diapers, wiping runny noses and bandaging knees. The hours spent sitting by the piano, helping a young mind to read music, the teenage years when Sara didn't even want to walk down the street with her parents. I sighed as I checked one of the web sites. Up on the left hand corner I noticed the word "Homestay."

I said aloud, "Let's click on that and see what that's all about." Minutes later, I wrote:

Dear Sir,

I am interested in a homestay program in southern France for the month of October. I speak some French, but my main goal is to become more fluent in the language. I am seventy-six years old, but I am very healthy. I like to hike, swim, garden and cook. Do you have something available, and how much is the cost?

Sincerely,
Janet Crawford

CHAPTER EIGHT
A MONTH IN PROVENCE

I had always kept a diary of our trips. My closet contains a box overflowing with little spiral memo books. The front of each one has the date and the destination. I retrieved the previous year's, the one that had "France 2007" on the front. There were only five pages with writing. I took the magic marker and added "2008." Like the previous year, I was expecting this trip to be radically different and I wanted to remember it as much as the previous ones.

The new page began, "I arrived after dark from Charles de Gaulle, Paris on the TGV, twenty minutes late. Jeanine and Louis met me. We drove near the center of Nimes to their small apartment. This is a temporary stay as my hostess, Josette, has two New Zealand girls with her at the moment."

"The flight was ten and a half hours, a stay at the Paris Gare was from eleven in the morning until 5:43, then on the TGV until eight. I remembered everything my friend, Anne, had showed me last year, about finding the right train and track. I wonder why I am here, why I decided to come back, pushed to return, even to strangers." I scribbled as tears filled my eyes. My sorrow was like a glass of tears, filled near the brim with a lid on it. Most of the time 'the lid' was covering my grief, but it was always so terribly close to the surface.

"Jeanine and Louis' pleasant features and happy smiles, along with several kisses on the cheek, cheered me up. I felt fatigue and depression slip from me, like water from a greased spoon. Kissing is a regular part of the greeting process. I loved it, but it took a little practice. At first, I found I was on the wrong cheek at the wrong time. After a couple faux paux, I decided that showing the left cheek first seemed to work the best. Kissing a woman's soft cheek was preferred. The men often had a little growth of whiskers which irritate. Kissing Dick, with his mustache and trimmed beard was like kissing a sea urchin; yet the kiss was worth it."

I ended the page much as I did last year except for the last several sentences. "I must admit that I long less for Dick as I struggle to pick up on every French word. Those who help me are patient, thank goodness! I took a walk up the road into a hillside area where it turns into a path. I picked a wild blue flower to put in my diary. Dick's grandmother called him 'Sweet William.' This will remind me of him. The night was filled with dreams of Dick."

Widowhood was still very new to me. I looked to others who have lost their mates. None seemed to feel as strongly about their loss as I did, although I'm sure this was an illusion. How long will these clouds of sorrow pass over me before there is just blue sky? How do I feel? Is it loneliness or helplessness? Is it a desire to re-live my youth, the time when our love was new? Or is it simply that the life I shared is no longer shared? Can I control these waves of emotion, these salty tears, the strange sound of someone crying that turns out to be me? Is it the touch of his hand, the feel of his chest touching me when we embraced? The sound of his heart beating when I laid my head against his body At night, when I felt the mattress shift next to me? When I expect two of us to solve a problem, decide on a movie, a trip to the store or one to the other side of the world? I miss his voice, but I have videos that solve that one, but do they? It is his words to me that I miss…but the other questions, perhaps there are no answers. Maybe it will be only time that dulls the pain, the tears, the sadness, the sorrow, the loss. I will have to wait and see. I don't have a choice. Maybe it is a fear that I will forget his face, his touch, his presence in my life.

———————

Four days later, I packed up my luggage and stepped into Josette's car. My long term homestay began. Josette, an attractive woman, greeted me with a smile that lit up her beautiful, yet sad eyes. She didn't speak any English, a perfect opportunity for me to immerse in French right from the start. We drove to her nice three bedroom house with tile floors and a large veranda that offered views over the whole valley. Cavairac, a little village near Nimes had a 12th century church, castle and fountain. The village was filled with ancient homes and tiny streets and I delighted at the prospect of spending a month there. Summer was reluctant to leave this part of France, since not much fall color was apparent. However, occasional rainy days prompted me to get out my drawing paper and Cray-Pas to pass the time. If I could just stay busy, interested in something, anything, I could keep my mind off of my sweet husband, but that was not easy to do. Whenever I tasted a special dish, a delicious Rhone wine, a wonderful soft goat cheese, these experiences would remind me that he wasn't there to share it with me. In spite of the language difficulties, the new location and new friends, Richard was never far from my thoughts.

I had another dream one night with the presence of Dick. I said to him, "But you are dead! I saw you take your last breath. I have your ashes in my bedroom." "No," he said. "I didn't die. I am still here. Rub my back." I took him in my arms and kissed him over and over, telling him how much I had missed him, and I rubbed his back. Like most dreams, in "real time" it was only a matter of a second or two, but dreams like that are so real and so emotional that they are never forgotten. For the time being, it was also the last one that I had that was associated with his death.

———————-

At sixty-four, Josette's energy and lovely smile helped me to settle in quickly. Her light brown hair curved pleasantly around her face and her sad eyes twinkled when she laughed. I considered her much younger, but then I considered myself in the same way. Soon, we felt the comfort of a growing friendship, and the "homestay" effect disappeared. If Josette needed to clean her house, I swept the veranda or helped with the laundry. I took Lolette, the delightful black, smooth-coated dog for a walk up the mountain roads. Above the valley and the villages, the landscape reminded me of Table Rock above the Rogue Valley in Oregon near my home. Here, silence, nature, and a rough stone path welcomed me for miles. The not-too-hot sun warmed my face and the pure air spurred me higher on the hikes. I had to admit that even if Dick were still alive, I would be doing this alone. He had given up wanting to climb hills and take walks as he aged, but I hadn't given up wishing for his presence.

I felt great delight speaking terrible French. Somehow Josette and her acquaintances figured out what I was trying to convey. I knew that I would never pass as a French woman. It was too late, too many years from my childhood. A homestay in France was not going to do the trick, but staying a month, just speaking and learning much more of the language was exactly what I wanted. I could almost hear Dick say, "Face up to it! Just enjoy what you can get out of this. You really don't have to prove anything to anybody!" However, I felt extremely pleased when, on two occasions while being introduced, the person said to Josette, "My, she speaks French!"

One day, the two of us visited a friend of Josette's. As I entered the house, I suddenly had this incredible feeling, a wave of latent emotion. I momentarily believed that the person I loved, whom I missed, whom I longed for, would be sitting in the living room on a chair waiting to surprise me. Logic told me this incredible event could not happen. But hope is not so easy to bury. Of course I didn't see Dick sitting there, but I sensed within me this wonderful scenario of the unbelievable joy, the scream that could be heard by all the Angels and Gods in the heavens, as I rushed to devour him with hugs and kisses. I struggled to maintain my demeanor during such an unusual moment. I almost felt like I was about to faint. Later I thought, "If there were such a moment... but only a moment...would it be worth it?" My answer was "no." For nearly a year, I had spent each day trying to cope with despair, depression and sadness. Although I felt less emotion when I was away from home, I still suffered from Dick's death every day. The thought of starting over with that painful process was not worth the one minute of joy. Yet, the feeling was so unexpected and unnerving, that it too, would remain with me, just as the dreams would.

The next day, Josette announced the venue for the last week. With Elmire, Josette's ninety-year-old mother, we would drive to Cannes and Nice, spending two nights at Josette's daughter, Nathalie's, apartment. This opportunity delighted me, since Richard and I had never been to this area of France. Typically, unless a tourist wanted to spend the "big bucks," costs there were "off limits." We enjoyed perfect weather as we walked along the beach. With joy, I took a nice swim in the just warm enough water and collected a few pounds of smooth pebbles. It amazed me that Elmire, who joined us on a long promenade by the shore, did so with ease. At meals, she ate heartily and polished off a glass of wine as well.

I found myself wondering, "What would Dick be like if he had lived to be as old as Elmire? Could he walk along this lovely shore? Would he enjoy this area?" I constantly had questions. At least the tears came with them less frequently. Perhaps I had succeeded in "solving" my sadness. Perhaps travel to new places with new faces provided an answer to my longing. I even found myself looking at men, wondering what it would be like to know someone new. But who would want me? I wouldn't be interested in anyone who was in his seventies. It would have to be someone much younger. I smiled at the thought that such a man would be interested in a seventy-six year old woman—not likely.

While in Nice, I had an idea. Josette had two cousins who lived in Corsica. I had met one of them at a family gathering near Avignon. Perhaps Josette and I could spend part of the fifth week of my trip in Corsica, since she had not visited them in many years. I had originally planned on going to Paris for several days before flying home, yet this seemed to be a great opportunity to see this beautiful island.

"Mais oui!" Josette grinned.

"That sure didn't take long!" I thought with a chuckle.

We purchased the tickets for the ferry after calling her cousins, who were anxious to see her. Josette would take her car so we could explore "Corse" From one end to the other.

We boarded the ferry at Marseille on a sea that looked quite calm, but wasn't. This massive ship carried cars, buses, semi trucks and trailers on the lower two levels. Josette and I had a cabin with two beds and a little bathroom with sink, shower and toilet. There were several large rooms where food and liquor was sold and entertainment was provided. Large areas, on two levels, were open to the fresh sea air where one could view the endless Mediterranean. The ship was clean, attractive and easily accommodated a large number of people on this regular route to Corsica.

After a ten hour ferry trip of mal de mer, where I barely survived not throwing up, we drove our car off the huge ship and found our way to a nice hotel overlooking the sea, just outside of Bastia. I recovered rather quickly from my nausea and was famished. I quite literally managed to devour a whole pizza at a small restaurant that night. The next day, we headed toward 'the cap' of Corsica, an area so delightful that I almost felt like finding a little house and moving there. The villages are tucked into the rugged coast with vistas to die for! Stone towers dot the coastline. They were built hundreds of years ago to watch for pirates and other hostile invasions. Part of the trip was through the mountains where Josette's driving was nearly as bad for me as the ferry trip.

After getting a hotel room in Calvi, we visited the huge citadel, bought some food and walked around the town as it started to sprinkle.

The following morning, a storm of major proportions descended with heavy rain, wind and later, fog. We left Calvi and headed into the mountains, and I do mean mountains! Josette's cousins lived a long distance from the coast. With nerves of steel, she insisted on driving over roads with mud and water gushing over them or brown waterfalls, from the mountainsides, pouring down onto the pavement. Parts of the narrow highway had been washed away and we passed a few cars that were in muddy ditches. The higher we went, the more fog we encountered. Sometimes we weren't sure where the road turned. It was white knuckle time for me, as the helpless passenger. I had to admire Josette's courage and determination. I was more than willing to find a little inn and discontinue the perilous trip.

On our safe arrival near the center of the island, Josette's cousins rushed out with umbrellas and escorted us into a lovely house, surrounded by fruit trees and flower gardens. I can't recall a time when I was happier to end a car trip! The house was full of warmth, both in ambiance, food and hospitality. Josette's speech suddenly revved up eighty notches! With me, she had spoken slowly. Now, she was with her cousins and other relatives. I managed to catch one word out of a hundred and that was only because she paused to catch her breath.

This was the eve of the US Presidential election, where every Frenchman I met hoped Obama would be elected. The following morning, I tip-toed down the tile steps, held my breath and turned on the TV, to the welcome news that Obama had won. I sat down and wept for nearly five minutes. It was not just because I had voted for him or the fact that Dick and I had been part of the Civil Rights movement. It was also because crying now came so easily to me. I could break into sobs over anything that aroused my emotions: a song, movie or other people's tragedies, even if I didn't know them personally, and it got worse the longer Dick was gone. I also had another problem. I was so used to hugging Dick that I had an incredible urge to hug whatever man I was around. He might have enjoyed it, but it was certainly out of the question for me to do it.

That evening, at the beginning of an incredibly delicious dinner, some very nice champagne was uncorked to celebrate Obama's election. The French television was full of the world's elation over his win. The coverage of this event continued throughout the day and into the evening. One would think that this was a French election instead of an American one.

The last day involved a drive toward the southern end of the island toward Bonifaccio. Although the island is part of France, the people have more than a little "Italiano" in both names of towns, people, food and language. I experienced an underlying local feeling of separatism. Richard would have wanted to engage someone in conversation, asking political questions. He never travelled to *just* view the scenery. Although he loved French and Italian food and wine, he also felt he was a student of the world. He wanted to look deeper, beyond the food and drink. From now on, I would have to do that for him. His influence on my travelling experience was palpable. Perhaps in this way it is true that he is still "here."

Returning to Marseille, Josette and I went to a large supermarche, where I purchased a large variety of cheeses and two bottles of Gaillac wine. Although Josette and I had drunk several bottles during my stay in Cavairac, I could not remember which of the many vineyards produced the wine that Dick had raved about. No matter, the special meaning of bringing back French wine counted. I planned to open a bottle with the Fords and then take one to Wisconsin at Christmas time to share with my family. Unfortunately, I hadn't taken into account the added weight to my luggage.

Soon after the shopping, we left for Aix en Provence and the

TGV station. The memory of my return trip the previous year hit me with a jolt of deep sadness. Yet this year's experience started out smoothly. Josette had made arrangements for my ticket before we had left for Corsica with the understanding that the destination should be Charles de Gaulle airport where Anne would be waiting for me. We both felt sad as Josette waited with me at the platform, our connection strengthened by broken hearts—Josette's two bad marriages and my Richard. In our time together, we had developed a warm friendship and both hoped that we would see each other again in the coming year. But *que sera*? We gave each other a long hug with many kisses on each cheek. I lugged my very heavy suitcase up the steep stairs, set it on a shelf by the exit, walked up the narrow aisle and found my allotted seat, placing a small green bag and my backpack on the shelf above. The train began to move before I could wave another goodbye.

CHAPTER NINE
WAS IT *HIS* VOICE?

During the trip from Aix en Provence, I sat near a French girl who had spent months in Ireland and England. When the train stopped at Gare Lyon and everyone began to take their luggage and leave, she explained that the train was not going to continue to Charles de Gaulle Airport, but to Brussels. I panicked at the thought of trying to find my way to the airport as I pulled down the beat-up pink and purple multi-repaired backpack and the green Perrier bag full of gifts from Elmire, Josette, Jeanine and Louis. I walked up the aisle to retrieve my terribly heavy suitcase and struggled down the narrow metal stairs to the platform of the Gare Lyon station. If I had managed to find my way around the world in the past, it usually had been with Dick by my side. Now, totally up to me, I had to calm my anxiety and solve problems by myself—easy enough to say, but I felt frantic!

"There is nothing to fear, but fear itself! ...Richard! Where are you?" Somehow an inner voice spoke to me. Was it his voice? "You can do this, Janet. You can do this!" In that moment of helplessness, I truly felt his presence, his patience and his strength, and felt less overwhelmed.

"How in the hell do I get to Charles de Gaulle? Where is a ticket counter? What do I ask for? Yikes!" I felt like I was drowning, only in a sea of people. I was totally unprepared. It dawned on me that I hadn't been strictly on my own for over a month. The only problem I had solved was how to find my way when walking the mountain trails above Cavairac. I hadn't driven a car or made a decision on which road to take. I had only acted as Josette's co-pilot, watching for highway and road signs. I had helped cook and shop at the supermarche, yet nothing had tested my ability to travel on my own or to use the French language on anyone but Josette, her family and friends. The damn suitcase weighed a ton as I boosted it up one stair at a time, people dashing past me. Four steps from the top, a young woman grabbed the case and carried it to the top before quickly departing. "Merci bien," I said, as she disappeared into the crowd.

French public transportation handles millions of people each day. The stations or *gares* are large and often with several levels. I heard loud speakers and saw changing signs and *voie* (train tracks), often numbered into the twenties. I could find places to buy food and coffee, newspapers and magazines. Marked exits and stairs led to another area of the same station or a metro tunnel. Surely, I could find a place to buy tickets. After feeling completely alone, helpless and lost, with hundreds of people bustling about me, after asking for a place to buy tickets and misunderstanding several responses, I finally stood in a ticket line hoping to get what I wanted. I also needed, desperately, to find a toilet. But that would have to wait, and wait I did. The line moved glacially. Finally, I pulled the appropriate euros from my front pants pocket. The amount required clearly glared at me from the black box with the red numbers: 8.10 Euros. I glanced down at my new one way ticket to Charles de Gaulle Airport, only to find that the earliest one had already left while I was waiting in line! The next would leave in two more hours.

"At least this should give me enough time to find the right voie and a toilet. I know that this is for an RER train and not a TGV," I said to myself, hanging on to what little confidence I could find. I felt like someone in "Les Miserables," a forlorn figure nearly out of hope. I walked all over the station, both passing time and acquainting myself with the layout. The area that had the voies for the RER trains was at the far end of the station. Twenty minutes before the scheduled departure time, one of the many large signs indicated the destination and the voie. With many others, I hustled down the tracks. I found a second class voiture and used all my strength to lift my suitcase onto the train.

"Next stop, next step in my life…Charles de Gaulle! What has Anne done? What did she think when I didn't arrive at 6:32 from Aix en Provence? Shit!!!" I exclaimed in English, hoping no one else heard me. More than ever, I felt my loss. The two of us, Dick and Janet, the modern day Hansel and Gretel, had traveled so much and were so used to taking turns solving problems, even a little one like watching the luggage while the other used the toilet. With him, everything seemed so much easier.

As I got off the train, my frustration quickly increased as I realized that all I had to connect me to Anne was email…no phone number, no address…nothing! For some reason, this didn't occur to me immediately. So, not knowing what else to do, I first stationed myself near the Information Booth. After a rather rude man left the kiosk, I asked the woman who replaced him and who looked like she had come from India, to please page Anne for me.

"Certainly, I'd be glad to," she said in English, in spite of my French inquiry. So much for my perfected French! But nobody came. I waited for nearly an hour hoping Anne would come back Finally, finally, finally, I realized the answer to my conundrum and wandered back to the Indian woman.

"Pardon, is there a place where I can use the internet?"

"Yes, take the escalator up two floors to the Sheridan Hotel. They have internet service. Perhaps they will let you use one of the computers," she graciously responded. I thanked her and followed the directions she had given me.

"Thank God for escalators!" I gasped, as I maneuvered the dead weight suitcase up and off the moving steps. The old wheels creaked on the smooth marble multicolored design outside of the posh entrance to the hotel.

"Maybe I could get a Metro ticket and find a hotel in Paris. That should be fun with all this damned luggage! If Dick were here, we would do it. Three days until I fly home. Well, give this a try. Maybe Anne will look at her email…I hope, boy do I hope!" I muttered as I walked into the upscale interior. I had a habit of thinking out loud, whether it was in my garden or a ritzy hotel in Paris.

"Bonjour madame, S'il vous plait, Je voudrais employer une ordinateur." I thought I did that quite well.

"Oui. Il y a cinquant euros pour une heure," came the sweet reply.

At that point, having recognized that the cost was fifty euros, I switched to English, explaining that I only needed the computer for one minute. Her smile welcomed my plea and she quickly got a key and led me over to one of the computers, turning it on for internet use. I thanked her in French—it had become a habit.

I took a deep breath and managed quickly to get to yahoo.

com. At seventy-six years of age, it was useless for me to ever think I could master the intricacy of this machine, but I kicked myself for not having all the right information for everyone I planned to come into contact with on my trip.

I guess I am a little like Blanch DuBois in a 'Streetcar named Desire' where I expect 'the goodness of strangers,' the optimism that everything will turn out fine and people who are supposed to meet me will arrive, no matter how the train and flight schedules screw everything up! I focused my thoughts back on the computer and pushed "reply" after I brought up Anne's last message. I began to write:

> Dear Anne,
> The ticket that was purchased for Charles de Gaulle by my friend, Josette, only went as far as Gare Lyon, so I had to get another ticket when I got there. I am now at the airport and I hope you read this email. I am very sorry that you made a trip to get me and I hope that you read this soon. I will be near the Information Booth.
> Love,
> Janet

A little while later, I saw Anne hurrying up to where I was sitting with all of my baggage. I leaped to my feet and we embraced. Every time we met, she appeared to be my "Guardian Angel."

"I am so glad to see you!" Anne sighed loudly. "I came and when there was no train, I asked the man at the Information Booth and he said that no trains starting with the number 6 come into this station. I thought about calling the police, but what could I tell them? I am so glad to see you!" Although I protested, Anne took the handle of the suitcase and began wheeling it toward an exit. "When I got home, not knowing what to do, I kept checking my email and then I found your message. I was so relieved!"

"Anne, I am so sorry you had to go to so much trouble. It would have helped if I'd had a cellular phone like everyone seems to have, but then I don't know your phone number." We both laughed, and continued to talk as we made our way out of the building into the dark Parisian night. At Anne's cozy apartment, she prepared some soup and the two of us talked until nearly midnight. Anne had to work for half of the next day. I suddenly felt energized after solving today's problems and proposed a trip to Chartres to see the cathedral. But Anne felt there wouldn't be enough time if I waited for her to return from work, so I decided to go alone. Anne drew up a little map showing me how to get to the train station, which was several blocks away, and then gave me instructions for the Metro.

After struggling through two harrowing train stations, I arrived at Chartres. The day wasn't pleasant with a cold wind and overcast skies. Yet, a nice warm husband, with his arm around me, would have made the day perfect. Just the thought warmed me. Such thoughts came to me constantly. I yearned for Dick to experience the fantastic Cathedral and all that I was seeing— the gorgeous stained glass and the incredible size of the twelfth century church. Maybe he was with me, not just in times of trial, but in times when I wanted him to share a special moment. I hoped so.

"Well, that turned out well," I thought, beginning to feel I had the situation under control. "Next time I come to France, I will spend more time in Paris and maybe travel to some other parts of the country. It's not that hard…well without the luggage!"

The train arrived to take me back to Gare Montparnasse. I

mistakenly got on going the wrong direction, but at the next stop, I quickly got off and went to the other side of the tracks. Once I found the right spot in the warren that is Montparnasse, Gare Haussman didn't seem so bad. Going back to Anne's apartment, I walked too far up the street before asking directions. Finding one's way around Paris was frightening and fascinating, a dialectic of emotions. It was another step toward my new life, a life that would require me to do my own problem solving.

Morning came all too soon. Before the lazy sun in the November sky had time to show itself, Anne brought her car around. I put the cheeses in my backpack, grabbed the Perrier bag and off we went to the airport. She had already put my suitcase in the trunk. Anne wanted to stay with me as long as possible, but finally gave up as the lines were huge. We parted as we had a year before, hoping to see more of each other in the future. What a gift to have met such a marvelous and kind person! If I lived in Paris, Anne would be a close friend. Now just the internet connection would continue to knit our friendship together.

After the long check-in lines finally relieved me of my bag, I stood in an even longer line after I entered the labyrinth of the security bottleneck. When it was over, I was in tears since all of my wonderful cheeses were thrown out; only the *dur* (hard) cheese from Corsica passed through security. Even though I had successfully brought some cheeses through in my backpack the previous year, the rules had apparently changed and I watched helplessly as my delicious cheeses got dumped in the trash.

"I should have put them in the suitcase! Oh damn! damn! damn! Not only did they cost me plenty of euros, but they're being wasted. I had so hoped to share some of them with the Fords and my family…and with myself." I wiped my eyes and nose but the depression continued. I kept weeping and wiping even after I had taken my seat on the airplane, even after we flew well over the British Isles. Perhaps it wasn't just the cheese. Perhaps the loss of the cheese triggered a realization of my hidden desire to return to France. I might never know why I felt such a strong pull to learn French. It really didn't make much sense, but I came to realize as I sat on that plane, forty thousand feet above the earth, why I was so desperate to return there on the exact date as last year. Deep, very deep within me, I now understood that I held within me an intense desire, a hopeless hope, that the end of this trip would be different. I would be coming back to San Francisco as I had planned a year earlier. I would step off the plane, anxious to see the Fords...and Dick, my wonderful Dick would be waiting with them.

"I'm just going to dissolve into their arms! I'll just cry until there's nothing left of me!" I whimpered. I walked to the toilet at the back of the plane and placed myself on the seat where no one could hear me cry. The engines drowned my sorrow. Finally, red-eyed, I made my way back to my seat. It was a turning point, although I didn't realize it at the time. I had finally come face to face with my lingering desire and hope that had even manifested itself in my dreams of Dick. Life was not a Greek or Shakespearean tragedy where all the main characters die but reappear to take bows at the end. Dick was not coming back and I was going to have to free myself from this hidden expectation.

I watched "Mama Mia" three and a half times before the plane landed. As I waited for my suitcase to come off the carousel, I looked at my pink and purple backpack, still part of my gear, but sadly devoid of cheese. What a shame! On the cart I had placed the green Perrier bag, full of gifts from my new found friends, those so-called "distant and disdainful" French who had opened their homes and hearts to me. I groaned as I lifted my suitcase off the metal belt and onto the cart, and headed out into the late morning sunshine.

It was a beautiful fall day in San Francisco. Flowers bloomed and birds still chirped in the tiny oasis of greenery used to soften the acres of concrete. The Fords drove up almost immediately and I gave them each a warm hug. The car drove away from the airport and turned north. Thirty minutes later, we found seats in the Buena Vista Bar, down where the cable cars start up the hill—where one can look out the window at the lovely gardens across the street, and beyond, the gray water of the bay. I ordered three Irish Coffees.

"Here's to Richard" I said. We raised the special glasses with the dark coffee, whisky and whipped cream topping. As I drank, I said to myself, or maybe, just maybe to him, "I love you, Dickie."

CHAPTER TEN
SEEING A LIGHT AT THE END

In February, I greeted my youngest son, Dan, at the Minneapolis airport. Traveling away from my despair seemed to be the best solution for my grief. Having one of my children with me was a wonderful bonus. Our camping trip with Nomad Tours, again with tents, began in Nairobi, Kenya. The first day, before we joined the tour, Dan and I walked from our hotel to the very nice Nairobi Museum. The displays were worthwhile, but we were especially impressed with the African bird collection. Of course, we got lost going back to the hotel and had to ask at least twenty people before we followed their advice and turned in the opposite direction. Everyone we spoke to was helpful and pleasant.

It was the rainy season, but that didn't stop us from seeing all the glorious animals and birds in the Serengeti and Ngorogoro Crater, including a pride of lions, with eighteen month old youngsters playing like two oversized kittens. It was obvious to me that my depression, with the help of my delightful son, was abating. It was ironic, because I probably would not have come to the south of Africa if Dick hadn't died and I wouldn't have conceived the idea of being here with each of my wonderful sons.

All visitors can only stay twenty-four hours in the Serengeti and Ngorogoro Crater. I could have stayed a month, if they had let me, just to have the time to identify the birds. Some were rather easy because they are so large, like the Sacred Ibis and the Malibu Stork, but the little ones, so full of color, were too quick to fly away or our special car just left them behind.

The larger animals, so content in their environment, made them more distinctive, so much different than in a zoo. We were delighted when a single giraffe came to the side of the road to drink from a puddle. She was accompanied by a group of zebras. Watching her bend her stilt-like legs to get a drink was quite exceptional.

Days went by quickly. At the camp site above the Ngorogoro Crater, an elephant came into camp to have a drink from the huge tank that supplied water for the kitchen and washrooms. In Luangwa National Park, a hippo nipped grass during the night just outside our tent. Earlier that day, during a game drive, we watched two hippos fighting over a female. We learned that they stay in the water during the day because their skin is so sensitive to sunburn. Where the water is too shallow for them to remain nearly submerged, they use their tail to throw water over their back. At night, they come ashore to graze on grass.

Dan and I saw lovely specimens of fish when we dived and snorkeled off the coast of Zanzibar. It was like diving in a huge aquarium, but then, that's what it is. As we traveled over roads meant for human and animal feet, our truck bounced and jerked mile after mile, but the people and animals we saw made up for all the misery of the potholes. As with all travel, it gives one an opportunity to understand and appreciate a part of our world that is both different, varied and unique.

I had always wanted to see the Masai tribe and I was not disappointed. Just the way they dress, wrapped in colors so bright, and their tall, thin stature, I saw them as works of art. Their cattle, too, are so lovely with the soft shades of gray, tan and brown and ivory.

Dan and I talked about Dick throughout the trip but we did it without tears and sorrow. Of course it makes a difference if the location is on a sandy beach by Lake Malawi, or a forest opening where we observed lovely flowers and equally beautiful birds. It was so nice to be with this happy and upbeat son, to share this trip and our love for each other.

After visiting unique places in Malawi and Zambia, we stood together, soaking ourselves in the rain and mist of Victoria Falls. Traveling for a month, our trip ended at Johannesburg, South Africa. We hugged, shed a few tears and boarded separate planes for Wisconsin and California.

Driving alone, to and from San Francisco, became less stressful. I no longer carried the anxiety I used to have. At the start of my trip in early February, I successfully drove from Oregon in a difficult snowstorm with thick ice on the road. I managed to put on and take off the tire chains and arrived exhausted at the Ford's house after a very long day. But I had made every turn onto every highway, just as Dick would have done.

At the end of March, I took a big step and explored dating. I would…could never find someone who fit me like Dick; nor was I expecting that to happen. It would just be nice to go to a play or movie, maybe a dance. I looked for a suitable man on one of the internet dating organizations, but not with much enthusiasm.

After one "coffee date," I put that idea away. Maybe there would be someone, maybe not.

The tears and waves of depression lessened, though I thought of Dick every day, often many times a day and many times an hour. I could understand now when grieving gurus talked about the stages of bereavement: denial and anger, then acceptance. But acceptance was the wrong word for me. There would never be acceptance; maybe it should be "no other choice." If I believed just a little bit more what Dick had said in my dream, it would be easier. When I poured a glass of wine, I raised it and toasted him. When I felt like talking to him, I did. No one was around to think I was loony. In my bedroom, I could look at his pictures, from all stages of his life, many with our entire family around him, and I didn't cry. Well, sometimes I did, but there were times when I could open the envelope that I kept on my chest of drawers, and sometimes, I could read every line. A couple of years earlier, while I was in Egypt with a friend, Dick had written this note and given it to me when I returned. It now brought me as close to him as I could ever get. I was so thankful that he had written it, that he put in writing how much he appreciated me. It was *almost* enough to get me through the ache of the sad days.

CHAPTER ELEVEN
DICK'S LOVE LETTER

February 2006

My dearest Janet,

If there has been any upside to our 1 month separation, I would say that it has given me time to reflect on just how fortunate and blessed I have been for the past 52 years. As I go about my prosaic activities it allows me to understand how unusual you really are. I find it to be slightly burdensome to accomplish just a fraction of what you routinely get done in a day. Just seeing that the dogs are let out, fed and put back in their cages in a timely fashion is just barely a fraction of your daily routine.

I look at the pictures of our children in our bedroom and I reflect on the fact that you had to get them clothed and fed daily for almost

25 years. What an accomplishment! And they turned out to be pretty nice adults. Just that alone qualifies as an outstanding achievement! As I think about the homes we have lived in and the effort and skill you brought to making them esthetically interesting, I can only think again how much you have added to my life.

As I watch the videos of you dancing, I'm reminded of how special it is that you managed to overcome your fears and inhibitions and become the skillful and accomplished performer that you are. I believe I am married to one of the most beautiful and ageless women I have ever met! Not only do you inspire erotic fantasies, you help make them realities. That alone makes me feel like one in a million.

Your varied interests throughout the course of our marriage are a constant and necessary ingredient in adding zest and delight to my existence. I hope you understand that even when disagreements occur they do not change my basic appreciation of who you are and what you mean to me.

In short, I hope that the good times continue to roll for as long as possible and that I love you more than you could ever realize. Thank you! Thank you! Thank you!

OLD DOG TREY

On the envelope was written one word: "Sweetness."

LOOKING BACK AND LOOKING FORWARD

It could have been one morning when the sun was shining, the grass was green and my garden looked beautiful, but it could have been when I was hiking on a mountain trail with nature all around me, or when I looked into the eyes of my beautiful children and grandchildren. Whenever it was, I felt the heavy burden of heartache and loneliness lift from me. I could have seen it coming if I had already written my story.

Laurie suggested I go to a meeting of Dave's Club, a new group for widowed people. I didn't think I needed it. Perhaps I didn't, but I found myself returning. I listened to the stories of others in the group. I heard their loneliness, sadness, suffering and even indecision. It was mostly the latter that struck me the most. All of us would go through the pangs of widowhood, but I could see a need to look in new directions, a need for self discovery. Maybe I could help them see that life could have purpose and even joy.

I often added some encouragement as the meetings continued. I could see that Sandy Baleria (whose inspiration started the group, named for her deceased husband) was bringing up some very good topics, ones that would give many in the group some hope and direction. From these discussions and my own experiences, I decided to put the following pages in my book. It is my hope that these pages will help others to step from confusion to find new directions for their lives.

PART THREE

RISING FROM OUR
HUSBAND'S ASHES

CHANGES

Despair is the only cure for illusion. Without despair we cannot transfer our allegiance to reality———-it is a kind of mourning period for our fantasies. Some people do not survive this despair, but no major change within a person can occur without it. —Philip Slater

It takes time for the initial misery to pass before one can be objective. We should look back on profound grief as a true indication of the love and affection shared between two people. It is a "badge of love and courage," one that a widow or widower should not hide or deny. Let yourself be sad, to cry, and depend on others when the going is rough. It is all right to be hugged by well-meaning friends and acquaintances, to let them take your hand and invite you into their hearts.

We should remember that the reason the sadness is so great is that two individuals, over the years, have become one entity. Breaking that bond is like severing a leg, only we have lost half of the person we were. We must heal like our bodies would. It takes time, lots of it.

Being the survivor is hard work. You are fighting incredible emotions that flood you throughout the day and night. Later, much later, the flood may hit in waves that are just as hard as before, but perhaps won't last as long. With all of this sorrow that most of us keep hidden from the world, we are supposed to work, laugh, keep the bills paid, see that the house is clean, take care of the lawn and pets and somehow present a picture of having made it through without much suffering or depression. You are living a secret inner life, one that cries out for release. You are in a prison and sentenced to hard labor. If we must accept death, we must also accept that we are in this for the long haul. Let's try and make the best of it, try to relieve the anguish and get on with our lives.

SOON AFTER THE OBITUARY, YOUR LIFE CHANGES

The reaction to the death of a spouse can manifest itself in many ways. There is no good or bad way for this to happen. It is an individual thing. I personally know of two people who quickly sold their house and furniture and moved to another state. Yet another one gave away her spouse's favorite chair and removed all of his personal pictures, art and books. There are those who disposed of the car or truck, the sports equipment or tools that were of no use to the survivor. The most common change was giving away his clothes and just keeping a few special garments, perhaps to give to children or grandchildren. Some do this one step at a time—just letting go of a shirt or a pair of pants, even finding comfort in wearing jackets, sweatshirts and sweaters of their loved one.

Physical changes to the environment may or may not take place. One widow told me she set his place at the table each evening. Others changed around the furniture in the living room or moved the sleeping quarters to another bedroom, making the old bedroom into an office or library. Getting rid of the old bed and buying a new one, often of a smaller size, is common.

Remodeling and repairs are also commonplace, some because they had been put off due to the sickness and death of the spouse, and other times to finally change something that always had been a bone of contention. A bereaved husband redid his wife's garden although he had never been interested in gardening before. It is a wise choice for some individuals to visit friends or family for several months, feeling the importance of having a surrogate person to help bridge the loss.

Others have a hard time with change. They may stop cooking his favorite foods or leave all of the clothes, shoes and belongings as if they expect him to return, walk down the hall or step in the door. They might see a car similar to the one driven by their loved one and expect to see him or her in the driver's seat. I avoided all of Dick's favorite restaurants, gave up ice cream and have no cable or television service. I also try not to drive down the street where the hospital is located.

Various individuals have other ways of coping, like going to places that both of them loved, spreading his ashes in those places or even in countries that he always wanted to visit. Some take a trip that the two of them had planned but never fulfilled. Many like to have all of his favorite furniture, books and pictures around them. Others take flowers and visit his grave frequently. Of course, this also goes for widowers who have lost their wives.

Most of us suffer from some degree of Post Traumatic Stress Syndrome for many months, or even years, after a spouse's death. In some individuals, it is quite severe, with uncontrollable trembling and inability to sleep or make decisions. Of course, there are other symptoms that may be equally severe. It is necessary to get professional help even though one might feel it is somehow a sign of weakness; that they must struggle through alone.

DISCOVER THE NEW YOU

This is not a panacea, but it can affect you in a positive way.

1. Change your hair style or hair color.
2. If you are a man, grow a beard or shave it off.
3. Leave the house wearing bright and pretty clothing that expresses who you are (or want to be).
4. Listen to jazz before you leave the house.
5. Listen to music when you're in the house.
6. Get a massage as often as you can afford it.
7. Try a new cologne or perfume.
8. Women, put on some makeup, brighten those lips.
9. Get new seat covers for your car.
10. Smile and get your teeth fixed.
11. Get plenty of exercise outside and/or join a local exercise club.
12. Eat healthy meals and take care of your body.
13. Be helpful to others. Volunteer.
14. Join clubs and groups that hold your interest.

ANOTHER LIFE CHANGE

Coping with loneliness, despair and depression—many choices.

1. Join a group that helps people who have lost a loved one.
2. Start a new activity or hobby by joining a class or college course.
   a. Community College Classes.
   b. Low-cost or free classes for Seniors.
3. Check out local volunteer groups for one that you may be interested in.
   a. School programs like 'Head Start" or playground supervisor.
   b. Pink Lady programs or other hospital volunteer work.
   c. Habitat for Humanity or Public Park volunteer.
   d. Working for a political party or candidate.
   e. Contribute time for stage work and plays or ticket taker.
   f. Volunteer for Red Cross work.
   g. Be a park host for a state or national park (summers).
   h. Humane Society helper.

  i. Working with disadvantaged children, battered women.

10. Visit your children, relatives and out of town/state friends.

11. Travel to places you have always wanted to go. Join a tour.

12. Continue hobbies and sports that take you away from the house.

13. Make new friends, meet for lunch, cook dinner for them.

14. Cultivate yourself by learning a new language, even traveling to a foreign country for a course.

15. Learn how to do the cha-cha or other Latin dances. It is FUN!

16. Consider taking a class for writing poems, memoirs or stories about your spouse's life.

17. Start a garden and join a garden club.

18. Become a bird watcher and join the Audubon Society.

19. Do activities that you loved but your mate didn't care for.

20. Begin to realize that making your own decisions on how to spend your time is rewarding (cook what you like, eat when you like and sleep as late as you like).

HOW TO LIVE IN AN EMPTY HOUSE

This can be a very difficult problem. It isn't possible to be active or away from home all the time, nor will family and friends always be present to brighten and fill your home with talk and laughter.

1. As mentioned before, listen to music that elevates your mood.
2. Avoid listening to news or political commentary that brings bad news into your head.
3. Purchase or rent some DVDs of favorite movies to watch in the evening.
4. Watch TV selectively, such as the Discovery Channel or Public TV.
5. Get a pet. A cat is easier than a dog and doesn't have to be taken outside. A bird is great, especially if it sings.
6. Get a dog and take training classes in obedience or agility.
7. Plan on a movie, or stage play once or twice a week.
8. Make a number of phone calls to relatives and friends.
9. Do some "chatting" on the internet.

BEDTIME AND ALL THOSE HOURS
BEFORE DAWN

For the first two years, this can be a very difficult time. It is common for many to have sleepless nights. These suggestions may help.

1. Your loved one is not the only person who has passed away. As soon as you lie down in bed, name ten different people who you knew or that were part of history who have passed. Name different ones each night.

2. Take several deep breaths and let them out slowly. At the same time, try to relax all parts of your body, starting with your toes. (This also helps if you're in labor!)

3. Expect that you will begin thinking, even if you are sure that you are sound asleep. There will be thoughts of moments in the past that you desperately do not want to think about. As a last resort, ask the doctor to prescribe a mild sleeping pill and use it only as needed.

4. Get up and read a book or watch a movie on TV.

5. Don't drink coffee or tea, or indulge in sweet treats in the evening.

6. Start a *MANTRA* for yourself. When your mind insists on thinking, try saying or thinking "Rom-e-go Ring-e-go" over and over and over and over and over. You may find that this or other mantras quiet the mind so that you can drift back to sleep.

RECOGNIZE DENIAL AND OTHER DEMONS

Denial comes in such a variety of forms. There are times when you may say, "If only I had known sooner," or "If only I had understood that he was dying," or "If only we had taken that trip that he always wanted to take," or "I didn't know that he was that sick," or "I know he was in a lot of pain, but I still wish he was here with me." Or these statements: "I can't believe he died," or "How could he leave me?" or "I wish I had known more about her sickness so I could have saved her," or "I know the doctors screwed up and let him die."

Losing a mate may bring about a great deal of self-examination, not just of the moment, but of the past. You may start examining your relationship with your parents or your siblings. You might delve into the feelings you had when you lost your mother or father. These things happened to me.

When I lost my father, I was sixteen and madly in love with a seventeen year old boy, sure I was going to marry him in the near future. I didn't, but what I did do was transfer the grief I had for my father to the young love that I lost at about the same time. It took me fifty years to figure out that the reason I didn't mourn my father's death was because I had transferred that overwhelming feeling of loss. It also took me a long time to realize that my dad's death had such a profound effect on my life. Because I had witnessed mortality, I suddenly wanted to make sure that I never wasted time. When I started college I went to summer school and graduated in three years. All of my children were born before I was thirty. If there was an opportunity available at the moment, I tried to take it because it might never be available again. I have lived a very rich and varied life and much of that can be attributed to my response to my father's death.

When Dick was taken to the hospital with a dissected aorta, I was as unprepared as most people are when faced with a life-threatening disease. Lots of thoughts filled my head, such as, "This can't be true," or "This can't be happening," or "There's got to be some mistake," or "Surely modern medicine can cure the problem."

Two years after his death, Sara asked me why I wasn't at the hospital, by his bed, as she had been. I couldn't answer in the moment, but have given it a lot of thought ever since. The first answer I found was that I am an activist. I try to solve problems—a part of who I am. I felt I just couldn't sit by his side if there was some way, somehow I could solve his health problems. I certainly tried. However, this was only part of the answer. It came to me after two and a half years.

The answer is denial. Dick had never been seriously ill. I had tried to keep Dick healthy, as if death could thus be avoided. Like someone just diagnosed with cancer, the person doesn't seem that sick. Dick didn't look sick. He sounded just fine. Only all the tubes and monitors seemed out of place. When his kidneys failed, he still looked healthy to me. I always felt that this was all a mistake, that he would be home soon, and when he came home, all the projects that he had intended to do would be completed, because I had done all of them for him. Spending countless hours just sitting by his bedside, as the TV monotonously jabbered on, did not seem necessary, especially since two of our children were there to keep him company. I strongly believed that the two of us would have plenty of time once he left the hospital.

The night before he died, he was a skeleton of his previous self, yet I still denied the inevitable. A couple of words are not enough to explain my experience of watching my mate descend toward death. As I reflected, I discovered a much older denial. For most of my life, I have avoided going to funerals. Seeing my father in a casket was extremely traumatic, long after I had given it much conscious thought. Avoiding funerals was my first form of the denial of death.

I denied death in other ways. I had raised generations of Shetland Sheepdogs, but always placed them after their show or breeding career was over because I didn't want to experience their deaths. What I had attempted to escape, I found later, was as severely devastating as I had remembered when I viewed my father for the last time. Yet death is part of life and though I have denied death for most of my life, it must be faced…for me and all of the rest of us that are left behind. The first step is to accept it, but for me, the "it" was not Dick's death. It is the acceptance that all things die: insects, plants, trees, dogs and cats, parents, exceptional people throughout history, and the people we love.

Does recognition that all things die make it any easier? Is acceptance suddenly an elixir? Sorry, it is not that easy. A lifetime of avoidance, of denial, was just part of the grief process for me. I feel blessed that I can analyze myself, my behavior, my actions, but the deep devastating grief that I confront each day, each waking hour has only lessened with time. Still, two and a half years after Dick's death, melancholy, just as powerful, returns time after time. I have found respites when the world looks bright and cheerful, where friends help me forget, where hikes, horse rides and skiing make the experience a joy. But the depression often returns and no amount of denial or acceptance can ever erase the incredible void, the loss of a wonderful mate. However, facing the fact that you will remember and love your special person for the rest of your life doesn't mean that life can't be beautiful. Life *is* beautiful. Don't deny it.

TRANSFORMATION

If you read back starting with Chapter Four, you will begin to see changes in me as the weeks and months go by. Little by little, I began to gain confidence in myself. Longer periods of time would pass in between periods of gloom. The tone of my experience changed from shock and despair to feelings of loss and loneliness, then to wishing he was with me, wishing he could see what I was seeing or wishing he was part of my adventure. For me, the road to transformation was training my mind to deal with depression. I slowly willed myself not to "go there." I have experienced "trigger" dates, such as Christmas, Thanksgiving, anniversaries, birthdays, and the day he died. These are tough ones that I had to plan for: a visit with friends, a hike, a trip, even a movie. Being away from the house has helped, but the mind is stubborn and will not give up creating sorrow, grief and tears. Most of all, it insists on remembering moments that I want to forget, no matter how hard I try to block them. New triggers arise spontaneously . His picture or jacket, a passing ambulance, a song, street, restaurant or a newspaper article, to give you a few examples, quite suddenly dumped me back into despondency. It helps to put the pictures (or other objects) away until you find your tolerance has returned. Earlier, I talked about widowhood being similar to losing a leg and solving all the problems, pain and depression that would accompany that event. I leaned on my mate without even realizing it. I depended on him to help solve each day's problems and to participate in all of its pleasures. In order to now face each day, each problem, and each pleasure, I have to decide what kind of crutch I needed.

For me, the crutch became all of my activities, the friends associated with them, and the joy of travel. Obviously the love and caring behavior of my children and grandchildren greatly helped. Each person should think what form their own crutch will take and help to create it. Stop and make a list of your interests and your physical abilities. Try to match the two up with activities that seem to suit you best. The worst hole to fall into is the old demon, negativity, with thoughts like "I can't do that," or "No one would want me." Once you bridge that deep chasm, you will find that the world has much to offer. There are places, people or animals in every town that need your help. There are trips that can be done in a car to wonderful National Parks. Planes can carry you to fascinating locations. There are tours that will gladly include you as a single person.

TRY NOT TO SIT AT HOME AND FEEL SORRY FOR YOURSELF—LIFE IS TOO SHORT!

For many of us, the person we married joined us for most of our adult life. We may have entered marriage after high school or college, a time when we were with our family or a group of class mates. If you look back, you may discover that you have never been alone—until now. For those who have spent part of their life on their own, losing a mate and returning to being single may not be quite so difficult. I found that being my own person, making my own decisions and solving a multitude of daily problems has been a huge challenge, and not without plenty of low moments and tears. I kept looking for that someone who shared my life, my judgments, ideas, inspirations, and mistakes. Yet, there were moments and then days when I felt fulfilled, happy with my new-found freedom and pleased that I had conquered uncertainty. Now is the time for you, too, to discover your own persona, the person who is really you, THE PERSON YOU CAN BECOME!

You have witnessed death and dying. It was part of your life for days, months and often years. This is a "wake up call," a time to realize your life is finite. Don't put off doing the activities that will give you pleasure. "Pick yourself up, dust yourself off, change your way of living and if that ain't enough, then change the way you strut your stuff." Those lyrics are older than I am and arranged just a little bit different, but they still can work for all of us. Whatever happiness you can get, whatever you can squeeze out of each day, you will find that it will be a pleasure for you and your loved one who is still and always with you.

GO FOR IT!

*EXPANDING YOUR HORIZON
CAN CREATE A NEW PERSON
WHO IS NO LONGER AFRAID
OF HERSELF.*

Janet Jackson Crawford